The Golden Years of
SOMALIA

MOHAMED ALI HAMUD

Published by Be Published – Publishing Services

+61 450260348

Copyright © 2014 Mohamed Ali Hamud

All rights reserved under international copyright conventions. No part of this book may be reproduced, stored in a retrieval system, or transmitted in any form or by any means electronic, mechanical, photocopying, recorded or otherwise without written permission from Mohamed Ali Hamud.

Whilst every care has been taken to check the accuracy of the information in this book, the author and Be Published – Publishing Services cannot be held responsible for any errors, omissions or originality.

Acknowledgment

Authors know what he or she writes does not come freshly minted from their own personal and private thoughts they are an assemblage of words and ideas borrowed from other people. Fortunately I was in a position to learn from many, among those I would like to thank are my son Abdullahi Mohamed Ali Hamud for his support in collecting all data. My thanks also go to my daughter Asmahan Mohamed Ali she took a big part in arranging, organizing the layout of and planning of my book. Lastly, I would like to thank my daughter Rahma Mohamed Ali for her help in typing. Without help, commitment, patience and encouragement from my three children, this book would most certainly not have been written.

Contents

Introduction	1
Chapter one	5
Sultanates that existed in Somalia prior to colonization	
Chapter two	27
Potsdam Conference	
Chapter three	33
European Colonial powers competing for Somalia	
Chapter four	41
Dervish State from 1900 to 1920	
Chapter five	49
Trusteeship and the road to Independence	
Chapter six	59
Independence and Unification 1960	
Chapter seven	69
The Golden Years of Somalia (1970 - 1977)	
Chapter eight	83
Somali Lost Dignity (After government collusion in 1991)	
Chapter nine	89
Self-Destruction and Lawless State	
Chapter ten	95
The Kuwait Crisis	
Chapter eleven	101
Economic History of Somalia	
Author's Biography	117
Mohamed Ali Hamud	
Curriculum Vitae	128
Mohamed Ali Hamud	
Reference	130

Introduction

I am not going to belabour the early history of Somalia or the ancient maritime history.

Dealing only with recent history particularly from 19th century until 20th century. In Chapter 1 the Sultanates which were established between 13th and 19th centuries are included and during this time major events occurred the First World War (1914—1918) and the Second World War (1939—1945). I will not talk about the causes and effects of the two wars and results that dramatically changed the history of the world. Each continuing for five years. When they ended the main powers who won the war, held a conference at Potsdam in Berlin in 1945 and participating were Russia the USA and the UK.

After the Berlin conference several European powers began the struggle for Africa. This inspired Mohamed Abdullah Hassan the Dervish leader to begin, what became one of the longest colonial resistance wars ever. This man struggled for twenty years against the foreign invasion in East Africa and Mohamed Abdullah Hassan was supported across the whole Horn of Africa.

Sir Mohamed A. Hassan says in a poem "The British have destroyed our religion and made our children their children". He soon emerged as "a champion of his country's political and religious freedom, defending it against all Christian invaders. Sir Mohamed A. Hassan had national vision and he called for the unity of Somalia, he believed in a great Somalia which I will describe to you.

The Sultanates were established

Warsangali in 13th century, Ajuuraan in 14th century, Galedi in 17th century, Majeerteen in 18th century and Hobyo in 19th century.

Encompassing north eastern and some southern parts of Somalia, the Horn of Africa and the ancient harbor city of Mudug.

On May 9, 1936, Mussolini proclaimed the creation of the Italian Empire, calling it the African Orientate Italians (A.O.I combining Ethiopia, Eritrea and Somaliland. The Italians made many investments into the infrastructure in the region, such as the Imperial Road between Addis Ababa and Mogadishu. Over the course of the Italian Somaliland's existence, many Somali's enrolled as troops and were regarded as a wing of the Italian Army's infantry Division. This was also the case in Libya and Eritrea. They were organized into a battalion, commanded by Major Alfredo Ferranti to defended Culqualber. This campaign lasted three months until defeated by the Allies. After heavy fighting, the Somali troops and the Italian carabineer received full military honours from the British. In the first half of 1940, there were 22 000 Italians living in Somalia. The colony was considered one of the most developed in East Africa, that was is in terms of the standard of living, mainly in the urban areas.

More than 10 000 Italians were living in Mogadishu, the administrative capital of the Africa Orientale Italian. New buildings were erected in the Italian architectural tradition.

By 1940, the Villaggio Duca degli Abruzzi in Jowhar (Sugar mills) had a population of 12,000 people of whom nearly 3,000 were Italians and Somalis. This area enjoyed a notable level of development with a small manufacturing area and with agricultural industries. In the second half of 1940, Italian troops invaded British Somaliland and cast out the British. The Italians also occupied parts of the British East Africa Protectorate bordering Jubal and around the towns of Moyale and Buna. In this regard I do not refer to the sultanates, which existed before the occupation of Italy like: Sultanate Majeerteenia Sultanate Hobyo, Sultanate Afgoye and Luuq Ganaane Grad Aw Mado.

This book is arranged as follows:
- The introduction
- The Sultanates that existed prior to colonization
- The Potsdam conference
- The European powers competing for Somalia, Dervish state,

established by Sid Mohamed Abdullah Hassan in 1900
- Somalia under Trusteeship
- Somalia's Independence in 1960
- The Golden years of Somalia from 1970—1977
- Somalia's lost dignity after the collapse of its Government
- Somalia's self-destruction
- The Kuwait crisis and the position of Somali delegation
- The economic History of Somalia
- Author Biography
- This covers the Somali history from 13th century to the present time.

Chapter one

SULTANATES THAT EXISTED IN SOMALIA PRIOR TO COLONIZATION

The Sultanates Warsangali Sultanate in the 13th century, Ajuuraan Sultanate in the 14th century, Geledi Sultanate in the 17th century, Majeerteen Sultanate in the 18th century and finally Hobio Sultanate in the 19th century.

I record them according to their seniorities by centuries and use them as examples.

1). Warsangali Sultanate

The Sultanate was founded in the late 13th century 1298.

The Capital of this Sultanate was Las Quray, its Government ruled by Sultan and Gerad.

The Sultanate was ruling north east Somali, at the height of its power and was one of the largest sultanate established in the territory, and included the Sanaag. The Sultanate was ruled by the descendants of the Gerad Dhidhin, the influential Sultan Mohamoud Ali Shire governed the Sultanate, who assumed control during some of its most turbulent years. The Akil Dhahar ruled south of Sanaag and some portions of the Bari region. In 1884, the UK established the protectorate of British Somaliland through various treaties with the northern Somali sultanate, including the Warsangali Sultanate.

I.M.Lewis in his book A Pastoral Democracy, a study of Pastoralist and Politics among the Northern Somali of the Horn of Africa, refers to the Sultan (from the colonial literature) as a 'man of unusual influence,' a 'man of mercurial image' and a 'man of unusual strength'.

Several Somali Sultanates existed in Somalia prior to the European imperialism of the 19th century, but the Warsangali Sultanate was the only one with a robust tax – based centralized administration. I.M.Lewis (2002).

In 1896, a challenge of leadership emerged between the father and son. The powerful Gerad Ali Shire's authority was declining and young Mohamoud Ali Shire (who had the unspoken support of the Isse Garad) sought to undermine the power of his father. Finally the dispute was settled by the proposal that Mohamoud Ali should become Sultan, while the father would remain Gerad. Later on, The Sultanate entered into an alliance with the Somali religious and nationalist leader Mohamed Abdullah Hassan's Dervish forces in an attempt to defeat Britain and Ethiopia. The two powers wanted control of the Somali peninsula.

The Rulers of the Warsangali Sultanate:

Over the period twenty-eight Sultanates ruled starting with Gerad DhiDhin completing with Sultan Saciid Sultan Abdisalaan 1997 until 2013.

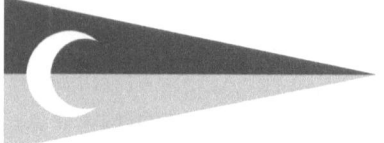

Flag of Sultinate of Ajuuraan

2) Sultanate of Ajuuraan

Established:	14th century
Decline:	17th century
The Capital:	Mareeg, Qaallafo and Merca respectively
Language:	Somali and Arabic
Religion:	Islam Sunni
System of Government:	Monarchy

It was a centralized state that ruled over large parts of the Horn of Africa in the middle Ages. Through a strong centralized administration and an aggressive military stance towards invaders, the Ajuuraan Empire successfully resisted both Oromo invasion from the west, whilst the Portuguese attacked from the east. This was during the Gaal Madow and the Ajuuraan Portuguese wars and the trading routes, dating from the ancient and early medieval periods of the Somali maritime enterprise. Because they were strengthened both foreign trade and commerce flourished, with ships sailing to and from many kingdoms and empires. Including; East Asia, South Asia, Europe, the near east, North Africa and East Africa. The empire left an extensive architectural legacy, of medieval Somali power, castles and fortresses. These are witnessed today in the many ruined fortifications that dot the landscape of Somalia.

Medieval Mogadishu was one of the most important states in the Ajuuraan realm. Attributed to Ajuuraan engineers examples include pillars tomb fields, necropolises and ruined cities built in that era. During this Ajuuraan period many regions and people in East Africa converted to Islam because of the theocratic nature of the government. The royal family, the house of Gareen, expanded its territories and established its hegemonic rule through a skillful combination of warfare, trade links and alliance. The Ajuuraan Empire monopolized the water resources of the Shebelle and Jubba Rivers.

Produced by hydraulic engineering, it was constructed with limestone wells and cisterns that are still in use today. The rulers developed new systems for agriculture and taxation, which continued to be useful in parts of the Horn of Africa as late as the 19th century. The tyrannical rule of the later Ajuuraan rulers caused multiple rebellions to break out in the empire, and at the end of 17th century, the Ajuuraan state disintegrated into several successor kingdom and states, the most prominent being the Ajuuraan Empire, which ruled over a territory that stretched as far inland as modern Qalafo and towards the coast, almost to Mogadishu. Said S. Samatar, writing with David Latin, noted that the Ajuuran sultanate represents one of the rare occasions in Somali history when a pastoral state achieved large—scale centralization'. He further noted that it grew larger and more powerful than the coastal city-states of Mogadishu, Merca and Baraawe combined.

Hobyo the ancient port of Somalia was the commercial centre of the Ajuuraan Sultanate. All commercial goods grown or harvested along the Shebelle River were brought to Hobyo to trade, as Hobyo remained the active mercantile pit stop of ancient times. The Ajuuraan rulers collected their tribute from the town in the form of sorghum (durra), making the port of Hobyo incredibly profitable to the sultans. Trade between Hobyo and the Banaadir coast flourished for some time. So vital was Hobyo, to the prosperity of the Ajuuraan Sultanate that when local sheikhs successfully revolted against the Ajuuraan Sultan and established an independent Imamate of Somalia, the power of the Ajuuraan sultans crumbled within a century.

Due to Portuguese predations, internal discord, and encroaching nomads from the north, the Ajuuran sultanate disintegrated at the end of the 17th century. According to Said Samatar, almost a full century passed before a successor state emerged: the Geledi Sultanate, which was based in the town of Afgooye and ruled over the lower Shebelle region.

Meanwhile, the Sultanate of Oman of South Arabia ousted the Portuguese from the Benaadir coast and ruled with what Samatar describes as a 'light hand' until the European scramble for Africa in the 1880's. As long as the Somali cities paid their yearly tribute (which was by no means extortionate) flew the Omani flag, accepted Omani over lordship, all were allowed to prosper. The Omanis allowed the Somalis to run their Omani governors in Mogadishu, Merca and Baraawe they were largely ceremonial. If the Omani authority was challenged, the Omanis could be severe. 'In the 17th century, Somalia fell under the wave of the rapidly expanding Ottoman Empire, who exercised control through handpicked local Somali governors. In 1728 the Ottomans evicted the last of the Portuguese occupation and claimed sovereignty over the whole Horn of Africa region. Their exercise of control was fairly modest as they demanded only a token annual tribute and appointed an Ottoman judge to act as a kind of Supreme Court for interpretations of Islamic law. By the 1850's Ottoman power was in decline.

The House of Gareen Known
Ajuuraan Gareen
Arliqo Gareen
Sarjelle Gareen
Fadumo Gareen
Umur Gareen

The house of Gareen was the ruling family of the Ajuuraan Empire whose origin lies in the Gareen Kingdom that ruled over Ogaden in the 13th century. With the migration of Somalis from the Northern Somali peninsula to the Southern Somali peninsula, this wave brought new cultural and religious orders that influenced the administrative structure of the Dynasty. With this new system of governance evolved an Islamic government.

Through their genealogical Baraka, coming from the saint Ballad (who was known to have come from outside the Gareen Kingdom), the Gareen rulers claimed supremacy and religious legitimacy over all other groups in the Horn of Africa. Ballad's ancestors are said to have come from the north western Somali city of Berbera.

Administration

Mogadishu was one of the most important client states in the Ajuuraan realm. The Ajuuraan rulers, instead of using the traditional Somali titles for the rulers, like Boqor or Sultan retained the title of Imam. In the Ajuuraan State, these leaders were the highest authority and counted multiple Sultans, Emirs and Kings as clients or Vassals. The Gareen rulers had seasonal palaces in Mareeg, Qaallafo and Merca, which they would periodically visit to practice primary notes. Other important cities in the empire were Mogadishu and Barawa. The State religion was Islam and thus law was based on Sharia.

The structure of governance is as follows

Imam:	Head of the state
Amir	Commander of the armed forces and navy
Na'ibs:	Governors
Wazirs:	Tax and revenue collectors
Qadis:	Chief judges

Nomadic citizens and farming communities

The Gareen rulers controlled the region's wells and effectively held control over the nomadic subjects. Large wells were carved out of limestone and were constructed throughout the state. These attracted Somali and Boran nomads for their livestock. The centralized regulations of the wells made it easier for the nomads to settle disputes by taking their queries to government officials who would act as mediators. Long distance caravan trade, a long time practice in the Horn of Africa, continued unchanged in Ajuuraan times. Today, numerous ruined and abandoned towns throughout the interior of Somalia and the Horn of Africa are evidence of a once booming island trade network dating from the medieval period.

The farmers

Farms in the Jubba Valley and Shebelle Valley increased their productivity. A system of irrigation drains known as Kelliyo fed directly from the Shebelle and Jubba rovers into the plantations where sorghum, maize, beans, grain and cotton were grown during the Gu and Xagaa seasons of the Somali calendar. This irrigation system was supported by numerous sandbags and dams. To determine the average size of a farm, a land measurement system was invented with moos, taraab and guided, being the terms used.

The system of Taxation

The State collected esteem from the farmers in the form of harvested products like durra, sorghum, bunand from the nomads of cattle, camels and goats herders. The collecting of tribute was done by a

Wazir (minister). Luxury goods imported from foreign countries were also presented as gifts to the Gareen rulers by the coastal sultans of the state.

A political machine that was implemented by the Gareen rulers in their realm was IUS primae noctis, which enabled them to conduct marriages that enforced their hegemonic rule over all the important groups of the empire. The rulers would also claim a large portion of the bride's wealth, which at the time were 100 camels.

Urban and maritime centres

The Sultanate ports became profitable trade outlets for commodities originating from the interior of the State. The farming communities of the hinterland brought their products to the coastal cities, such as Mogadishu, Merca and Barawa, where they were sold to local merchants who maintained a lucrative foreign commerce, with ships sailing to and from Arabia, India, Venetia, Persia, Egypt, Portugal and as far away as China. Vasco Da Gama, who passed by Mogadishu in the 15th century, noted that it was a large city with houses four or five levels high, big palaces in its centre and many mosques with cylindrical minarets in the 16th century. Duarte Barbosa noted that many ships from the Kingdom of Cambaya sailed to Mogadishu with cloths and spices, for which they in return received gold, wax, and ivory. Barbosa also highlighted the abundance of meat, wheat, barley, horses, and fruit on the coastal markets, which generated enormous wealth for the merchants. Mogadishu, the centre of a booming weave industry known as toob benadir (specialized for the markets) in Egypt and Syria, together with Merca and Barawa also served as transit stops for Swahili merchants from Mombasa, Malinda and for the gold trade from Kilwa. Jewish merchants from the Hormuz also brought their Indian textile and fruit to the Somali coast in exchange for grain and wood.

Economy

The Ajuuraan Empire and its clients were active participants in the East Africa gold trade and the Silk Road commerce.

Trading coins from several Asian kingdoms and empires have been found in Somalia, while Mogadishu coins have also been found in parts of the Middle East. Trading routes dating from the ancient and early medieval periods of Soins. Somali maritime enterprise were strengthened or re-established, foreign trade and commerce in the coastal provinces flourished with ships sailing to and coming from countless kingdoms and empires in East Asia, South Asia, Europe, the Near East, North Africa and East Africa. The merchants of the Ajuuraan Empire, with the use of commercial vessels, encompassed multiple port cities and lighthouses.

Mogadishu imported valuable gold Sequins coins from the Venetian Empire.

With several centers of global trade domain situated along the busiest trade routes of the medieval world, the Ajuuraan Empire and its clients were active participants in the East African gold trade the Silk Road Commerce.

Trading coins from several Asian kingdoms and empires have been found in Somalia, while Mogadishu coins have also been found in parts of the Middle East Trading routes dating from the ancient and early medieval periods of Somali maritime enterprise strengthened or re-established so foreign trade and commerce in the coastal provinces flourished with ships sailing to and coming from a myriad of kingdoms and empires in East Asia, South Asia, Europe, the Near East, North Africa and East Africa.

The merchants of the Ajuuraan Empire through the use of commercial vessels, compasses, multiple port cities, light houses and other technology did brisk business with traders from the following states:

Trading countries in Asia

	IMPORTS	EXPORTS
Ming Empire	celadon wares and their currency	horses, exotic animals, and ivory

Trading countries in Asia

	IMPORTS	EXPORTS
Mughal Empire	cloth and spices	gold, wax and wood
Malacca Kingdom	ambergris and porcelain	cloth and gold
Maldive Islands	cowries	musk and sheep
Sri Lanka	cinnamon and their currency	cloth

Trading countries in the Near East

	IMPORTS	EXPORTS
Ottoman Empire	muskets and cannons	textiles
Safavid Persian Empire	textiles and fruit	grain and wood

Trading countries in Europe

	IMPORTS	EXPORTS
Portuguese Empire	gold	cloth
Venetian Empire	sequin	
Dutch Empire		

Trading countries in Africa

	IMPORTS	EXPORTS
Mamluke Egyptian Empire		cloth
Adal Empire		
Swahili World		

Trading countries in Africa

	IMPORTS	EXPORTS
Monomopata	gold and ivory	spices and cloth
Gonderine Empire	gold and cattle	cloth
Merina Kingdom		

Ajuuraan State Culture

The Ajuuraan's facilitated a rich culture combining various forms of Somali culture such as architecture, astronomy, festivals and art all evolved and flourished during this period. The Somali war like art Istunka birthed during this period. Carving, known in Somalia as Qoris, was practiced in the coastal cities of the empire. Many wealthy urbanites in the medieval period regularly employed the finest wood and marble carvers in Somalia to work on their interiors and houses. The carvings on the mihrabs (prayer niche) and pillars of ancient Somali mosques are some of the oldest on the continent. Artistic carving was considered the province of men, similar to how the Somali textile industry was mainly a woman's business. Amongst the nomads, carving, especially woodwork was widespread and could be found on the most basic objects, such as spoons, combs, and bowls, but it also included more complex structures, such as the portable nomadic house, the aqal.

The empire left an extensive priceless architectural legacy.

Muslims migration to Ajuuraan realm

Many Arab and Persian families would call the Ajuuraan Kingdom their home. Therefore, the late 15th and 17th centuries saw the arrival of Muslim families from Arabia, Persia, India and Spain to the Empire, the majority of whom settled in the coastal provinces. Some migrated because of the instability in their respective regions, as was the case with the Hadhrami families from Yemen and the Muslims from Spain fleeing investigation while others came to conduct business or for religious purposes.

Due to their strong tradition in religious learning, the new Muslim communities enjoyed high status among the Somali ruling elite and commoners, frequently employed as religious advisers, in administrative positions or serving in the Ajuuraan army as soldiers and commanders.

The Sultanate Military

The Ajuuraan Empire had a standing army with the Gareen imams and the governors ruling and protecting their subjects. The bulk of the army consisted of Mamluke soldiers who did not have any loyalties to the traditional Somali clans system, making them more reliable. The soldiers were recruited from a well-known area; other recruits came from the surrounding nomadic region. Arab, Persian and Turkish mercenaries were at times, employed as well. In the early Ajuuraan period, the army's weapons consisted of traditional Somali weapons, comprising of; swords, daggers, spears, and bows. Thereafter, with the import of firearms from the Ottoman Empire, through the Muzzaffar port of Mogadishu. Horses used for military purposes were raised in the interior, and numerous stone fortifications were erected to provide shelter for the army in the coastal districts. In each province, the soldiers were under the supervision of a military commander known as an emir and the coastal area and the Indian Ocean trade was protected by their navy.

The war between Sultanate, Portuguese and Oromo invasion.

The Ottomans regularly helped the Ajuuraans in their struggles with the Portuguese in the Indian Ocean.

Portuguese empire war

The Portuguese empire (on the coast of East Africa), at the time enjoyed a flourishing trade with foreign nations. The wealthy south eastern city states such as Kilwa, Mombasa, Malinda, Pate and Lamu were all systematically sacked and robbed by the Portuguese. Tristao da Cunha then set his eyes on Ajuuraan Territory, where the battle of Barawa was fought. After a long period of engagement, the Portuguese soldiers burned the city and looted it. However, fierce resistance by the local population and soldiers resulted in the Portuguese's failure to permanently occupy the city. The inhabitants who had fled to the interior would eventually return and rebuild the city. After Barawa, Tristao, the commander of Portuguese soldiers, would set sail for Mogadishu. This was the richest city on the East Africa coast. However word had spread of what had happened in Barawa, and a large troop mobilization had taken place. Many horsemen, soldiers and battleships, in defensive positions guarded the city. Nevertheless, Tristao still opted to storm and attempted to conquer the city. Against the approval of his officer and soldiers who feared certain defeat if they were to engage with their opponents. Tristao then heeded or considered their advice and sailed for Socotra instead.

In 1660, the Portuguese in Mombasa surrendered to a joint Somali – Omani force. Over the next several decades Somali Portuguese tensions remained high and the increased contact between Somali sailors and Ottoman corsairs worried the Portuguese. In return they sent a punitive expedition against Mogadishu under the Commander of Joao de Sepulveda, which was unsuccessful. Ottoman – Somali cooperation against the Portuguese in the Indian Ocean reached a high point in the 1580's when Ajuuraan of the Somali coastal cities began to sympathize with the Arabs and Swahilis under Portuguese rule and then sent an envoy to the Turkish corsair Mir Ali Bey for a joint expedition against the Portuguese. He agreed and was joined by a Somali fleet, which began attacking Portuguese colonies in Southeast Africa. The Somali - Ottoman offence managed to drive out the Portuguese from several important cities such as Pate, Mombasa and Kilwa. However, the Portuguese governor sent envoys to Portuguese India requesting a large Portuguese fleet. This request was answered and it reversed the previous offensive of the Muslims into one of defense. The Portuguese armada managed to re-take most of the lost cities and began punishing their leaders, but refrained from attacking Mogadishu. Throughout the 16th and 17th centuries successive Somali Sultans defied the Portuguese economic monopoly in the Indian Ocean by employing a new coinage which followed the Ottoman pattern, thus proclaiming an attitude of economic independence against the Portuguese.

Oromo Invasion

In the mid 17th century, the Oromo Nation began expanding from its homeland around Lake Abaya in southern Ethiopia towards the southern Somali coast. This was at the time when the Aluuraan Empire was at the height of its power. The Gareen rulers conducted several military expeditions known as the Gaal Madow wars against the Oromo warriors, Islamizing those that were captured. The Ajuuraan Empire's military supremacy forced the Oromo conquerors to reverse their migrations towards the Christian Solomonids and the Muslim Adalites, devastating the two warring empires in the process.

Decline

The Ajuuraan Empire slowly declined in power at the end of the 17th century. This happened due to the dethronement of the Muzzaffar clients in Mogadishu and the imposing of high taxation on the citizens'. The Somali maritime enterprise took a hit after the collapse of the Ajuuraan Empire. However, other Somali polities replaced the Ajuuraan State such as the Warsangali Sultanate, the Gobroon Dynasty, the Majeerteen Sultanate, the Dervish state, and Sultanate of Hobyo.

Conclusion

The Ajuuraan State was a modern state, due to its ordered and hierarchical structure such as: Imam (the head of the state), Emir (commander of the armed forces and Navy), Naibs (governors), Wazirs (ministers who administered the state), Qadis (represent of the judicial system). This system is according to contemporary states. This Sultanate did not have a parliament system. (Wikipedia, 2013)

3) Geledi Sultanate or Gobroon Dynasty

This was established in the late 17th century and abolished late 19th century.

Its Capital was Afgooye, its language was Somali and Arabic, its religion was Islam Sunni and the system of Government was Monarchy.

Geledi Sultanate was a Somali Sultanate that ruled parts of the Horn of Africa during the 17th and 19th centuries. The Sultanate was governed by the Gobroon Dynasty. It was established by General Ibrahim Adeer, who was General in the Ajuuraan Army. It was he who defeated various Vassals of the Ajuuraan Empire and founded the house of Gobroon.

The dynasty reached its peak under the successive supremacy of Sultan Yusuf Mohamud Ibrahim who successfully consolidated Geledi power during the Bardera wars, and Sultan Ahmed Yusuf who forced regional powers such as the Omani Empire to submit to the mark of respect. At the end of the 17th century, the Ajuuraan Sultanate was in decline and various Vassals were now breaking free or being absorbed by Somali powers. One of these powers was the Silci Kingdom, which began consolidating its rule over the Afgooye region. But the General Ibrahim Adeer led the revolt against the Silci ruler Umar Abroone and his tyrannical daughter, Princess Fay. After his victory over the Silci, Ibrahim Adeer proclaimed himself Sultan and subsequently started the Gobroon Dynasty. Ibrahim and the other Gobroon nobles were descended from Cumar Diine, an early Muslim leader who had arrived with four of his brothers from the Arabian Peninsula. Among this group of siblings, all of whom were Islamic clerics, was Fakr ad- Din. The First Sultan of the Mogadishu Sultanate in 13th century. The Geledi army numbered 20 000 men in times of peace, and could be raised to 50 000 troops in times of war. The supreme commander of the army was the Sultan and his brother, who in turn had Malaakhs and Garad under them. The military was supplied with rifles and cannons by Somali traders of the coastal regions that controlled the East Africa arms trade. (Virginia, 2002)

The Gelled clan has lived for about 400 years in the town of Afgooye on the Shebelle River, the origin Afgooye. There is a story that says, when the Sultan of Silci saw his defeat and said "Affray gooey – afkooda Allah ha gooey" that means in English "they cut my mouth, may Allah cut their mouths". This is the origin of the name of Afgooye.

The rulers of the Geledi Sultanate.

General Ibrahim Adeer Established the Geledi Sultanate in the late 17th century, the first ruler in the Gobroon Dynasty.

Mohamud Ibrahim inherited the throne from his father.

Yusuf Mohamud Ibrahim's Rule marked the start of the Golden age of the Geledi.

Ahmed Yusuf Mohamud regularly extended support to East Africa Sultanates.

Osman Ahmed Yusuf Inherited the throne from his father marking the beginning of the decline of the Sultanate.

4) The Majeerteen Sultanate

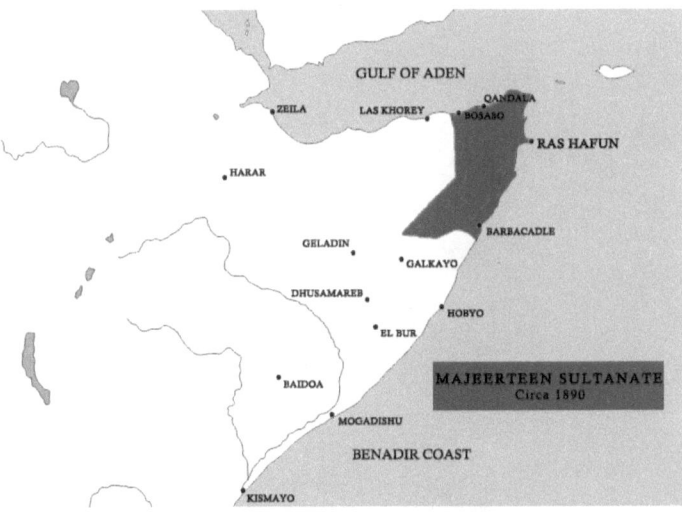

The Golden Years of Somalia

The Majeerteen Sultanate was Established mid-18th century and it was in decline early 20th century:

Capital: Alula Bargal (Seasonal)

Languages: Somali-Arabic

Religion: Islam

Majeerteenia Sultanate was a Somali sultanate on the Horn of Africa, ruled by King Osman Mahamud. During its golden age, it controlled much of northern and central Somalia in the 19th centuries. The polity had all of the organs of an integrated modern state and maintained a robust trading network. It also entered into treaties with foreign powers and exerted strong centralized authority on the domestic front. It rose to prominence the following century under the reign of the resourceful Boqor (King) Osman Mahmud.

Due to consistent shipwrecks along the north eastern Cape Guardafui headland, Boqor Oman's kingdom entered into an informal agreement with Britain, wherein the British agreed to pay the King annual subsidies to protect shipwrecked British crews and guard wrecks against plunder. The agreement, however, remained ungratified as the British feared that doing so would give other powers a precedent for making agreements with the Somalis, who seemed ready to enter into relations with all comers.

Majeerteen-Italian treaties

In late 1889, Boqor Osman entered into a treaty with Italy, making his kingdom a protectorate known as Italian-Somaliland. Both Boqor Osman and Sultan Kenadid had entered into the protectorate treaties to advance their own expansionist goals.

The rulers also hoped to exploit the rival objectives of the European imperial powers so as to more effectively assure the continued independence of their territories.

The terms of each treaty specified that Italy was to steer clear of any interference in the sultanates' and their respective administrations. In return for Italian arms and an annual subsidy, the Sultans conceded to a minimum interference and economic concessions. The Italians also agreed to dispatch a few ambassadors to promote both the sultanates and their own interests. The new protectorates were thereafter managed by Vincenzo Filonardi through a chartered company. An Anglo-Italian border protocol was later signed 5 May 1894, followed by an agreement in 1906 between Cavalier Pestalozza and General Swaine. This last protocol acknowledged that Baran fell under the Majeerteen Sultanate's administration. With the gradual extension into northern Somalia of Italian colonial rule, both Kingdoms were eventually annexed in the early 20th century. (Horn of Africa Journal, 1997)

As with the Sultanate of Hobyo, the Majeerteen Sultanate exerted a strong centralized authority during its existence, and possessed all of the organs and trappings of an integrated modern state: a functioning bureaucracy, hereditary nobility, titled aristocrats, a state flag, as well as a professional army.

However, the Majeerteen Sultanate's ruler commanded more power than was typical of other Somali leaders during the period. As the primus inter pares, Boqor Osman taxed the harvest of aromatic trees and pearl fishing along the seaboard. He retained prior rights on goods obtained from shipwrecks on the coast. The Sultanate also exerted authority over the control of the woodland and pasture land, and imposed both land and stock taxes.

In the early 19th century, Somali seamen on the northern coast blocked entry to their ports, while engaging in trade with Aden and Mocha in adjacent Yemen using their own vessels.

According to official reports from 1924 (commissioned by the Reggio Governo della Somalia Italiana), the Majeerteen Sultanate maintained robust commercial activities before the Italian occupation of the following year. The Sultanate reportedly exported 1 056 400 Indian Rupees (IR) worth of commodities, 60% of which came from the sale of frankincense and other gums. Fish and sea products sold for a total value of 250, 00 IR, roughly equivalent to 20% of the Sultanate's aggregate exports. The remaining export proceeds came from livestock, with the export list of 1924 consisting of sixteen items.

Military

In addition to a strong civil administration, the Majeerteen Sultanate maintained a regular army. Besides protecting the polity from both external and internal, military officials were tasked with carrying out the King's instructions. The latter, included tax collection, which typically came in the form of the obligatory Muslim alms (seko or sako) ordinary tithing by Somalis to the poor and religious clerics (wadaads). (Metz, 1993)

5) Sultanate of Hobyo

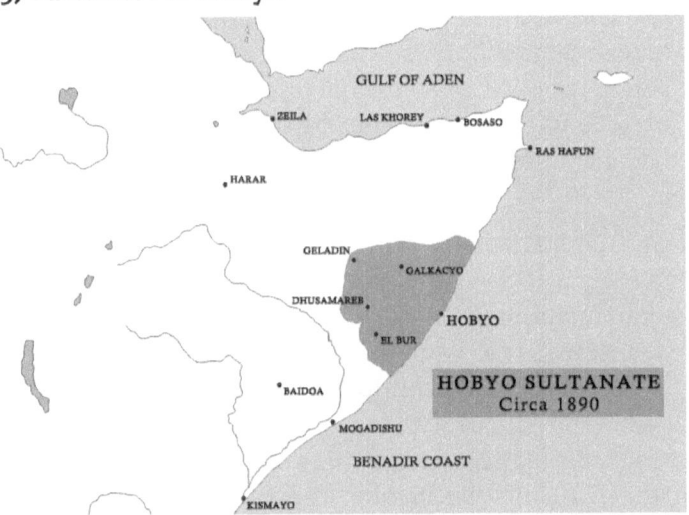

This was established 1878, by Sultan Yusuf Ali Kenadid, its Capital was Hobio, Languages: Somali and Arabic, Religion Islam Sunni, System of Government Monarchy. Also known as The Sultanate of Hobio, it was imprinted out the former Majeerteen Sultanate.

Yusuf Ali Kenadid was cousin of Boqor Osman Mohamud the Ruler of the Majeerteen Sultanate. Yusuf's goals were to seize control of the neighbouring Majeerteen Sultanate, which was then ruled by his cousin Boqor Osman Mohamud. However, he was unsuccessful in this attempt. After almost five years of battle between Boqor Osman and Yusuf Ali Kenadid (his ambitious cousin), Yusuf Ali Kenadid was exiled into Yemen. A decade later, in 1870's, Kenadid returned from the Arabian Peninsula with a band of Hadhrami musketeers of devoted lieutenants. With their assistance, he managed to overpower the local people of Hobyo. In late 1888, Sultanate Kenadid entered into a treaty with the Italians, making his realm an Italian protectorate. His rival Boqor Osman signed a similar agreement in respect of his own Sultan the following year. Therefore, both rulers signed the protectorate treaties to advance their own goals. With Sultan Kenadid looking to use Italy's support in his on-going power struggle with Boqor Osman over the Majeerteen Sultanate, as well as his dispute with the Sultan of Zanzibar over an area bordering Warsheikh. Both rulers also hoped to exploit the conflicting interests among the European imperial powers that were then looking to control the Somali peninsula, so as to avoid direct occupation of their territories by force. However, the relationship between Hobio and Italy worsened when Sultan Kenadid refused the rise and fall of the Sultanate.

Italy's proposal to allow a British contingent of troops to land in his Sultanate so that they might then pursue their battle against the Somali religious and nationalist leader Mohamed Abdullah Hassan's Dervish force was viewed as too much of a threat by the Italians. Sultan Kenadid was eventually exiled to Aden in Yemen and then to Eritrea, as was his son Ali Yusuf, the obvious heir to his throne. Omar Samatar's Rebellion in November 1925 to January 1926, he was one of Sultan Ali Yusuf's commanders and he attacked and captured El-Bur on 9 November. The local population supported Omar. Soon enough the Italians had a full scale revolution on their hands after Omar followed up his previous success with the capture of El-dhere. The Corpo Zaptie tried and failed to recapture El—bur from Omar. By 15 November the Italians had fled to Bud Bud, were constantly ambushed by partisans and were diminished in force and revolve. A third attempt was planned, but before it could be executed the commander of operation, Lieutenant – Colonel Splendoreli was ambushed and killed between Bud Bud and Bula Burde. Italian morale hit rock bottom and Hobio seemed a lost cause as Omar stood poised to reconquer Hobio itself. In an attempt to salvage the situations, Governor De Vecchi requested two battalions from Eritrea and assumed personal command. The rebellion soon spilled over the borders into the Benadir and Western Somaliland, Omar grew increasingly powerful. The disaster in Hobio shocked Italian policymakers in Rome. It was the Adwa fiasco of the first Italo-Ethiopia war all over again, and Italy's plans for East Africa were unraveling before their very eyes. Blame soon fell on Governor De Vecchi, whose perceived incompetence was blamed for Omar's rise. Rome instructed De Vecchi that he was to receive the reinforcement from Eritrea, but that the commander of the Eritrean battalions was to assume the military command and De Vecchi was confined to Mogadishu and limited to an administrative role. The commander was to report directly to Rome, bypassing De Vecchi entirely.

As the situation was extremely confused, De Vecchi took former Sultan Ali Yusuf with him to Mogadishu. Mussolini vowed to reconquer all of Hobio and move on to Majeerteen by any means necessary. Even reinstating Ali Yusuf was considered. However, the clans had already sided with Omar Samatar, so this was not as viable an option as it appeared.

Official Stamp used by Sultan Ali Yusuf Kenadid for correspondence with the other rulers in the Indian Ocean area and Europe.

Before the reinforcements arrived, De Vecchi chose the age old tactic of divide and rule and offered great rewards, money and prestige to any clans who chose to support the Italians.

Considering the eons-old clan rivalries, which have been the bane of Somali states from time immemorial, it is a wonder this strategy had not been attempted sooner, and turned out to be far more successful than the Eritrean regiments in reversing the rebellion.

With the steam taken out of the rebellion, and the military forces heavily reinforced with the battalions from Eritrea, the Italians retook El—Buur on December 26, 1925, and compelled Omar Samatar to retreat into Western Somaliland. (Metz, 1993)

Chapter two

POTSDAM CONFERENCE

This conference was held at Cecilienhof, The home of Crown Prince Wilhem HohenZollen, in Potsdam from July 28 to August 1, 1945. The Participants: were the Soviet Union, the United Kingdom and the United States. The three powers were represented by Communist Party General Secretary Joseph Stalin, President Harry S. Truman, Prime ministers Winston Churchill, and later Clement Attlee (whilst awaiting the outcome of the UK 1945 general election and The Labour party's victory over the Conservative). The conference decided what punishment to administer to the defeated Nazi Germany, after having agreed to unconditional surrender nine weeks earlier, on 8 May 1945 surrender NAZI.

They came to the following conclusion:

"The Governments of the UK, USA and the USSR considered it necessary to begin without delay the essential preparatory work upon the peace settlement in Europe. To this end they agreed that there should be established a council of Foreign Ministers of the Three Great Powers (France joined the big three) to prepare treaties of peace with the European enemy States, for submission to the United Nations. The council would also be empowered to propose a settlement of the outstanding territorial questions in Europe, they also considered other matters.

Political Principals:

In accordance with the Agreement, each of the three governments took control of a portion of Germany's interests and its own Zone of occupation in matters affecting Germany.

The agreement:

There shall be uniformity of treatment of the German population throughout Germany.

The complete disarmament of German troops, war machinery and control of all German industries.

War criminals shall be arrested and brought to trial.

The production of arms, ammunitions and all types of aircraft was to be prohibited.

The three big powers submitted a plan to rebuilt Europe.

To strengthen, the three big powers recognized a Polish Provisional Government of National Unity. The UK and USA, Governments had taken measures to protect the interest of a Polish Provisional Government of National Unity as the recognized government of the Polish State as well as the property belonging to the Polish State located in their territories and under their control.

All Nazi laws, as promulgated by the Hitler regime, of discrimination on the ground of race, creed, or political opinion were abolished. No such discrimination, whether legal, administrative or otherwise was to be tolerated.

All members of the Nazi Party who had been more than nominal participants in its activities, and all other persons hostile to Allied purposes were removed from public and semi—public office and from positions of responsibility in private undertakings. These people were replaced by people who by their political and moral qualities, were deemed capable of assisting in the development of genuine democratic institutions in Germany.

The Judicial system was reorganized in accordance with the principles of democracy, of justice under law and of equal rights for all citizens without distinction of race, nationality or religion.

The administration in Germany was directed towards the decentralization of the political structure and the development of local responsibility.

The German Navy shall be divided equally among the three big powers being the USSR, the UK and USA.

Reparations: The three big powers divided between them the following annexation and the regeneration of Germany:

The USA and UK, the zone of which they occupied.

The USSR to settle the reparation claims from the Zone occupied by the USSR.

The goals of the conference also included the establishment of post-war order, peace treaties issues and how to counter the effect of the war.

(Look at Wikipedia, free encyclopedia)

The division of Africa by European powers

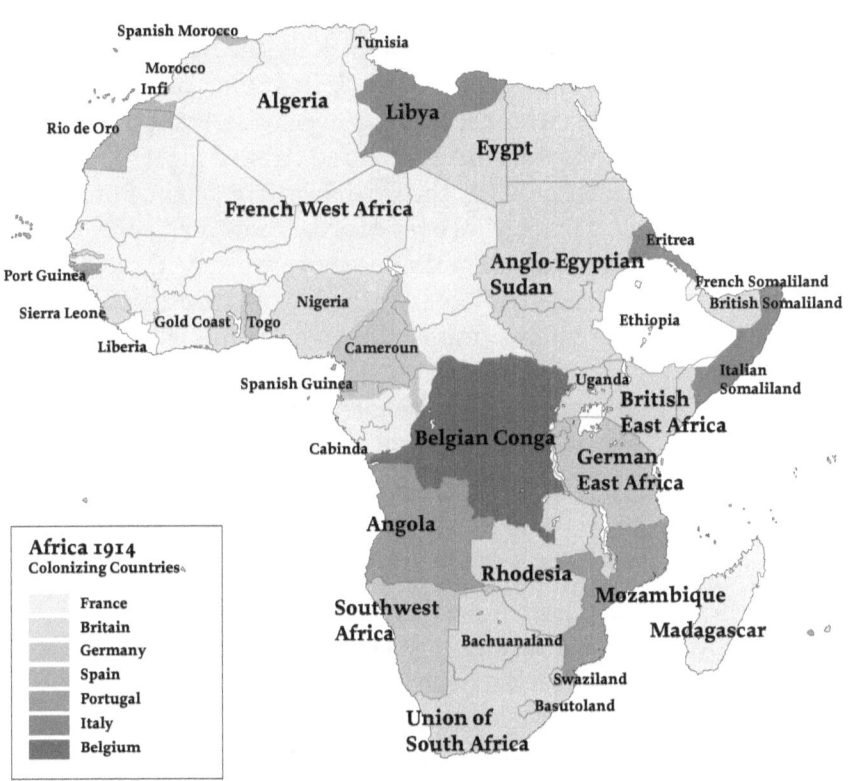

In 1884 at the request of Portugal and the German Chancellor Otto Von Bismarck they summonsed the major western powers of the world to negotiate and end confusion over the control of Africa. Bismarck appreciated the opportunity to expand Germany's sphere of influence over Africa and desired to force Germany's rivals to struggle against one another for territory, whilst at the same time, to build his own military and to invade European countries. This policy was successful.

At that time, greedy acquisitive European leaders were searching for minerals and markets had become their aim. At the time of conference, 80% of Africa remained under Native Traditional and local control. The countries represented at the time included fourteen countries or nations such as: Austria, Hungary, Belgium, Denmark, France, Germany, Great Britain, Italy, the Netherlands, Portugal, Russia, Spain, Sweden and the United States of America. Within these countries were the four major players; France, Germany, Great Britain and Portugal who controlled most of colonial Africa at the time. After the Berlin conference the European powers struggled to gain control over Africa. A new map appeared of the continent, which was superimposed over the one thousand indigenous cultures and regions of Africa. The new countries lacked reason and divided coherent groups of people and merged together disparate groups. All this was at the expense of the indigenous people. By 1914, the conference participants had fully divided Africa among themselves into fifty unnatural and artificial States.

By doing so, Europeans divided Africa and drew borders and maps, without taking into account local geographic condition and the ethnic composition. Nor were African leaders invited to participate.

The British prime minister of the time, Lord Salisbury (Sally), put it infamously: "We have been engaged in drawing lines upon maps where no white man's feet have ever trod; we have been giving away mountains and rivers and lakes to each other, only hindered by the small impediment that we never knew exactly where the mountains and rivers and lakes were"

The struggle for Africa started in the late 19th century and was fully completed by the turn of the 20th century. During the conference principles were laid down that would be used by Europeans for all Africa continents. The three major principles that emerged from the Berlin Conference were:

First: the hinterland (surroundings) doctrine, according to which power claiming the coast also had a right to its interior. The applicability of this principle became problematic, as it was not clear what exactly constituted the hinterland.

Second: the principle of effective possession required of Europeans needed to base their claim on the treaties with local tribe leaders.

Third: the effective occupation doctrine required that European powers use significant control of the territory they were claiming. This principle was soon diminished to apply mostly in the coastline, due to the insistence of the British. This conference, despite its importance, completely marginalized the African leaders to the basic economic strategic and political interest of European Power. As you can see in the map, Italy occupied Somalia, Eritrea and Libya. During the colonial period of dominance, the Somali people were divided between British, Italian and Ethiopian rule.

The political climate of the rest of the world often had a large effect on African colonies, especially Somalia. During World War Two the rivalry between the Axis and the Allied powers in Europe also had an effect on the social and political climate among the Somali people. (Naval History & Heritage, 1945)

Chapter three

EUROPEAN COLONIAL POWERS COMPETING FOR SOMALIA

From 1839—1897, the European powers contested for Somalia — all wanting to conquer it. But the question was; who would win Italy, Britain or France? The Europeans interest in Somalia increasing after 1939, when the British begin to use Aden, on the south coast of Arabia as a coaling station for ships on the route to India. The British defence force required red meat and the easiest local source was on the Somali coast. The same reason was pertinent for France and Italy. They also needed coaling facilities to power their ships and wanted to establish stations in the northern Somali regions. The French developed Djibouti. The Italians were a little further up the coast at Aseb in Eritrea. Such was the land grab for Africa, beginning in the 1880's, where all three powers competed for Somalian territory. Soon they were joined by a fourth rival, Ethiopia, where Menelike 11 became emperor in 1889. France and Britain, after a brief risk of armed confrontation, agreed in 1888 on a demarcation line between their relatively minor shares of coast. The French region around Djibouti became formally known as the French coast of Somalia and commonly referred to in English as French Somaliland. This remained a French colony until Djibouti became independent on 27, June, 1977 thus named the republic of Djibouti.

British influence in the coastal area around Zeila and Berbera was formalized during the 1880's in a series of treaties promising protection to the chieftains of various local Somali clans. The region became a protectorate under the title of British Somaliland. France and Britain had thus acquired control over two valuable stretches of coastline due to their increased commercial importance. This became even more strategic when the Suez Canal opened. But by that time the largest part of Somalia was disputed between Italy and

Ethiopia. Italy agreed to spheres of influence with Britain in 1884, placing the border between British Somaliland and Italian Somalia just west of Bender Qassim. At that time there was a disagreement between Italy and Ethiopia concerning the Eritrean treaty which rapidly soured relations between Italy and Ethiopia. By 1896 the treaty resulted in war between Italy and Ethiopia, and the Ethiopian army defeated the Italian at force Aduwa. This event weakened the Italian position. Therefore, Ethiopia was granted the west Somalia (Ogaden), and was ceded the Haud. In the intervening years the most dramatic upheaval occurred in British Somaliland, where the uprising led by Mohamed Abdullah Hassan (known to the British at the time as the Mad Mullah) took two decades to suppress.

A new era of conflict began in Somalia in 1923 with the arrival of the Italian colony of the first governor appointed by Mussolini, the newly appointed fascist dictator. A vigorous policy was adopted to develop and extend Italian imperial interest, culminating in the defeat of Italy and annexed to Ethiopia in 1936. Tension increased when the Second World War began. Then Somalia and Ethiopia were known as Italian East Africa.

By 1940 the British had withdrawn from their colony, while French Somalia claimed neutrality in keeping with the policy of the Vichy government or French government. However, in 1941, British forces recovered the entire area (except French Somalia) from the Italians, thus uniting (almost) the entire territory of the Somali people under British rule. Meanwhile French Somalia was being blockade by the allies. In 1942 the local administration changed allegiance and threw its lot in with the free French.

Between 1948 and 1950 the situation returned to the colonial boundaries as agreed in 1889. Ethiopia retained West Somalia and the Haud. French and British Somaliland continued as before. In 1950 the Italians return to Somalia under a UN trusteeship, with the commitment to bring Somalia to Independence within ten years.

Somalia and its strategic location:

Why did the three powers compete for Somalian territory? The answers follow:

Somalia has the longest shoreline in Africa and fishing was a very important source of income, as was tourism. At the peak of the Cold War, Somalia took advantage of its strategic location, that of strategic importance gained by the competing East and West fractions. This is why at some time during the seventies; it had the largest army in Africa. At that time Somalia enjoyed influence among African nations in many areas and had a strong military and strong economy. Therefore, Somalia had a powerful position on the international arena.

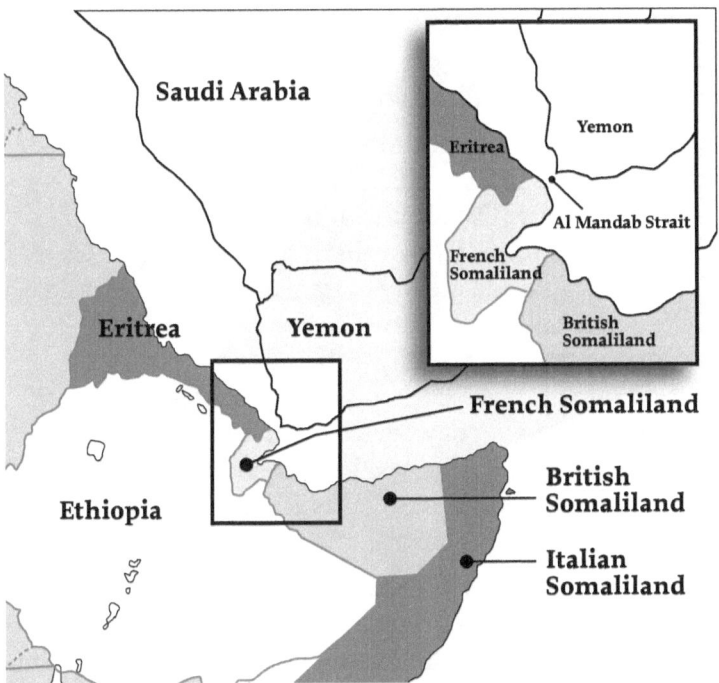

Bab Al Mandab Strait: (Gate of Tears)

Somalia is one of the states located in Bab al Mandab, which was an important place of trade between India and Western Countries and as a transit checkpoint. But since the opening of the Suez Canal and connection of the Red Sea with the Mediterranean Sea it became very important to all international countries as a southern gate of the shortest and quickest waterway linking the Indian Ocean with the Mediterranean Sea - therefore attention focused on the Strait of Bab al Mandab.

Entrance to the Red Sea, with the west of the world resulted in political, economic and military advantage to all nations.

The important of the Bab - al Mandab Strait

The Bab Al Mandab strait (12° 34' 34" North, 43° 21' 11" East) separates Africa and Asia connecting the Red Sea to the Indian Ocean via the Gulf of Aden. This strait is strategically important because it is considered one of the world's major oil transit checkpoints. The strait is about twenty miles (32 km) wide.

Much of Europe's crude oil from the Middle East passes through Bab al Mandab. Closure of the strait could keep tankers from the Persian Gulf from reaching the Suez Canal and Summed pipelines complex thereby diverting them around the southern tip of Africa (the Cape of Good Hope). This would add greatly to transit time and cost and effectively tie up spare tanker capacity. The Bab al Manda could be bypassed (for northbound oil traffic by utilizing an east and west crude oil pipeline, which traversed Saudi Arabia and had a capacity of about 4.8 million barrels per day. Security remains a major concern of foreign firms doing business in the region, particularly after the French flagged tanker Umburg was attached off the coast of Yemen by terrorists in October 2002.

Bab- al Mandab gained additional strategic importance as a result of the events of September 11, 2001; when the US had developed significant military and intelligence centres in Djibouti and Somalia as part of its effort to prevent attacks from Al- Qaeda in the Bab al Mandab region.

The British having been the preeminent regional power until the mid-1960 traditionally sympathized with the Somalia vision of national reunification. After being offered Western aid to equip and arm 5 000 men (sufficient only for internal security) Somalia accepted a Soviet offer of a $32 million loan and assistance in equipping and training a 10 000 strong armed force. Compared with Somalia's total military budget of $3.9 million in 1964 this was a windfall.

While the United States was involved in the Vietnam War, President Johnson decided to cut off aid to Somalia. Prior to these developments, Moscow supported certain Somalia policy positions- anti colonialism and opposition to foreign bases in Africa and to aggressive military alliances.

The major involvement in Somalia was undertaken when Moscow's difficulties with Sudan and Egypt (leading to the expulsion of Soviet advisers from both) as well as increased Chinese competition, underlined the importance of a friendly progressive regime in Somalia.

Close Soviet-Somalia relations brought about the transportation of Somalia's Kismayu train and Barbera port into the Soviet Union's main base facilities in the region. The investment into Barbera port had been worthless since the beginning when the Soviets enjoyed access to port facilities in Yemen, prior to being evicted from their Egyptian bases in the Red Sea.

Summarising why the European powers competed for Somalia?

Somalia has the longest shoreline in Africa (the Indian Ocean) where its fish, rich waters and contiguous international waters etc.

Somalia is one of the States which is situated in Ban al Mandab strait. This strait was strategic for political, economic and security reasons.

This strait links west to east through its gateway to the Indian Ocean

And through it passes 4.8 million of barrels of crude oil, from the Middle East to Europe daily.

Keeping your Navy stationed near Bab al Mandab was important in order to control this vital area.

Any political upheaval could disrupt the flow of oil shipment through the strait, which would impact not just this region but on all countries dependent on the oil transported through Bab al Mandab.

Division of Somalia: The big European colonial powers divided Somalia to take bits and pieces and split it in the following five different Somalian regions:

The so-called British Somalia: In 1839, the British Empire established a military protectorate in the North region, cutting it up from Somalia. It remained under British rule until independence in 1960.

The so-called French Somalia: In 1860 the French Empire decided to take one part of Somalia, which became independent in 1977, now known as Djibouti.

The so-called Italian Somalia: In 1889 Italy opted for not falling behind other European powers making the decision to occupy another part of Somalia. This is the large area positioned in the south and east of the Country. In 1938, Italy decided to enlarge its occupation and invaded other regions of Somalia, occupying west Somalia (Ogaden), which was under British rule.

This is the map of Somalia which was occupied by Italy in 1889.

The so-called Northern District Frontier (NDF); this region was annexed to the British ruled Kenya, before Kenya's independence from Britain. In 1963 this region decided to integrate into Somalia through a referendum. However, the result was declared null and it remained in Kenya.

The so-called West Somalia or Ogden Region: 1938, formally occupied by British, then by Italy and finally, it was annexed to Ethiopia. Somalia became independent in 1960 but some lands were lost or annexed to neighbouring countries. Therefore the European colonial powers created massive problems for Somalia and the region. They also created many problems in other parts of the world, such as Kashmir between India and Pakistan, and the like.

Chapter four

DERVISH STATE FROM 1900 TO 1920

Introduction

The Ethiopia Emperor Menelik sent an expedition to Somalia consisting of an army of 11,000 men, they made a deep push into the vicinity of Luug in Somalia. However, troops were soundly defeated by the Gobroo Army and only 200 soldiers returned alive. Ethiopia subsequently refrained from further expedition into the interior of Somalia. Nevertheless, they continued to oppress the people in west Somalia (Ogaden) by plundering the nomads of their livestock, numbering in the hundreds of thousands. The British blockade of firearms to Somalis rendered the nomads in the Ogaden helpless against the armies of Menelik.

With the establishment of important Muslim orders headed by Somali scholars such as Sheihk Abdurahaman bin Ahmed Al-zaylai and Sheihk Awais al Barawi, a rebirth of Islam in East Africa took place. The resistance against the colonalization of Muslim lands in Africa and Asia would inspire a large resistance movement in Somalia. Mohamed Abdullah Hassan travelled to many Muslim centers in the Islamic world returned to Somalia as an educated man and began promoting Salihiya order in the urban cities with major success.

He was born in April 7, 1856 in the Valley of Sa'Madeeq Somalia, some say he was born in Kirrit in northern Somalia. At this time, this part of Somalia was a protectorate of the UK (1884 and 1960) known as British Somaliland.

Youth

Sayid Mohamed Abdullah was the eldest son of Sheikh Abdullah, his mother was Timiro Sade, his grandfather Sheikh Osman of Bardee who left his homeland towards Qalaafo along the Shebelle River valley. From there he migrated southwards to settle with the religious Somali community at Bardheera along the Jubba River.

His grandfather, Hassan Nur, in turn left his home and moved closer to north eastern Somalia. There, he founded several religious centers and devoted himself to the worship of God. Sayid Mohamed grew up among pastoralists who were good herdsmen, warriors and they used camels as well as horses. By the age of eleven he had learned the Quran off by heart and displayed qualities of a promising leader and fine horseman. He continued his religious education. In 1875, his grandfather died. Sayid Mohamed was shocked by this loss.

After 1975, he worked as a Quranic teacher for two years. His thirst for Islamic learning was so intense that he left his job and devoted about ten years to visiting many famous centers of Islamic learning including Harar, Mogadishu and even centers in Kenya and Sudan. In 1891 he returned to his home and married. Three years later, along with two of his uncles and eleven other companions some were his maternal kin, he went to Mecca to perform Haji. The party stayed there for a year and half and came under the charismatic influence of the newly developing Saalihiya order under the leadership of the great mystic Mohamed Salih who was a Sudanee. Sayid Mohamed received initiation and very rigorous spiritual training under Salih.

Religious mission: in 1895 Sayid Mohamed returned to Berbera, which was under British control to gain regular supplies of meat from Somali through this port for their British India outpost of Aden. In Berbera, Sayid Mohamed did not succeed in spreading the teaching of the Saalihiya order because the local people were Qadiriah and they did not like this new teaching.

In 1897 Sayid Mohamed Abdullah Hassan left Berbera. On his journey at a place called Daymoole he met some Somali children who were being looked after by a Catholic Mission. When he asked them about their clan and parents, the Somali orphans replied that they belonged to the "clan of the Catholic Fathers." This reply shocked him. He felt that the "Christian over lordship in his country, was tantamount to the destruction of his people's faith".

The Dervish State was established by Sayid Mohamed Abdallah Hassan, religious leader who gathered Somali soldiers from across the Horn of Africa and united them into a loyal army known as the Dervishes. The Dervish army enabled Sayid Mohamed to carve out a powerful state through conquest of lands claimed by the Somali Sultans, the Ethiopians and the European powers.

The Dervish State acquired ownership of the Islamic world as well as successfully repulsing the British forces four times, forcing them to retreat to the coastal region. Politically they also maintained relations with other authorities receiving support from the Ottoman and German empire. The Turks also named him Emir of the Somali nation and the Germans promised to officially recognize the Dervish State.

In 1900 Sir Mohamed Abdullah Hassan established the Dervish State in Illig. Later he moved from Illig to Taleex in heart of Nuggal where he built three garrisons of massive stone work and number of houses.

In 1899 some soldiers of the British armed forces met Sayid Mohamed and sold him an official Gun. When questioned about the loss of this gun, they told their superiors that Sayid Mohamed has stolen the gun from them.

On 29th March 1899, the British Vice Consul wrote a severe and insulting letter to him asking him to return the gun immediately. This enraged Sayid Mohamed so he sent a brief and curt reply refuting the allegation. This incident caused a clash with the British.

Struggling against foreign invaders

Essentially, the movement led by Mohamed Abdullah Hassan was an anti - colonial struggle. As the British began their Protectorate, he began to resist their colonial rule. In several poems and speeches, he emphasized that the British were infidels who were destroying Islam and making the children of Somalia into their own children. This was in partnership with the Christian Ethiopians who were sent to plunder the political and religious freedom of the Somali nation. He soon emerged in the eyes of many Somalians as a defender of his country's political and religious freedom against the Christians invaders. He issued a religious ordinance that any Somali national who did not accept the goal of unity of Somalia or who would not fight under his leadership, would be considered as unbeliever (kafir). He acquired weapons from Turkey, Sudan and other Islamic countries. He appointed his ministers and advisers in charges of different sectors of Somalia. He gave a clarion call for Somali unity and independence.

Said Mohamed A. Hassan organized his warriors (the Dervish movement) essentially of a military character, with rigid hierarchy and rigid centralization. He committed the first attack by launching his first major military offence (with his 1500 Dervish, equipped with twenty modern rifles) on the British soldiers stationed in the region.

He sent his representatives throughout the counties appealing for Somali people to join his movement and many responded to him enthusiastically.

Ethiopian expedition

In 1900 an Ethiopian expedition, which had been sent to arrest or kill Sayid Mohamed, looted a large number of camel trains from Somali nomads. In answering to this looting, Sayid Mohamed attacked the Ethiopian garrison at Jigjig on March 4 of that year and successfully recovered all animals. This success encouraged Sayid Mohamed and improved his reputation. Towards the end of 1900 Ethiopian Emperor Menelik proposed a joint action with the British against the Dervish. Accordingly, British LT. Col . E.J Swayne assembled a force of 1500 Somali soldiers by twenty-one European officers. They started from Burco on 22 May 1901, while an Ethiopian army of 15 000 soldiers started from Harar to join the British forces to crush the Dervish movement of about 20000.

During 1901 to 1904, the Dervish army inflicted heavy losses on their enemies. This success encouraged the cause, even for Somalis, who did not follow his ideology.

On January 9, 1904 on the Jidaale plain, the British Commander General Charles Egerton killed 7 000 Dervish. This defeated the force of Sayid Mohamed so his remaining men fled to the south of Somalia.

The death of Richard Corfield

Sayid Mohamed memorialized this action, in his poem, simply entitled "the death of Richard Corfield", he wrote: You have died, Corfield and are no longer part of this world, a merciless journey was your portion. When Hell destined, you set out for the other World. Those who have gone to heaven will question you, if God is willing.

Defeat

In the beginning of 1920, the British struck the Dervish settlement with a well-coordinated air and land attack, inflicting a stunning blow and defeat. The forts of Sayid Mohamed were damaged and his army suffered great losses. Again with the help of his patriotic poetry and charisma, he tried to rebuild his army and created the coalition of Ogaden clans gaining a power in the land once again. The British sent a peace delegation to him who offered him a government subsidy and a land grant in the west of the British Somaliland, where he could settle with his followers. He scornfully rejected the proposal and even raided the returning delegation. Then, smallpox or rinderpest or some kind of plague broke out in the area and about half of the Dervish died.

Death: On May 1920, Sayid Mohamed died of influenza at the age of 64. He had fought tirelessly for twenty years against foreign invaders.

Legacy

The Dervish legacy, you can see in the country's culture heritage in Somalia, its history and society. In memory of past heroes, the military government of Somalia erected statues, visible near Hotele Shabelle as icons. During 1901 to 1904, the Dervish army inflicted heavy losses on their enemies (the British, Ethiopians and Italians forces). This is the life of war, one day is yours and the other day is for others.

Sayid Mohamed produced both War and Peace poets involved in a struggle known as the Literacy war, which had a profound effect on Somali poetry and Literature. Sayid Mohamed Abdullah Hassan featured as the most prominent poet of the age. In the 1920 campaign by the British, twelve aircraft were used to support the local British forces. Within a month, the British had occupied the capital of the Dervish state and Sayid Mohamed Abdulla Hassan has retreated to the west of Somalia. (Wikipedia, 2013)

Chapter five

TRUSTEESHIP AND THE ROAD TO INDEPENDENCE

Before we talk of trusteeship, we will analayse which governments, Italy or Britain were to be the choice of the UN for Somali trusteeship. Britain had control from 1950 until 1960 all over the Somalian Country then the Allied Army took over; 1941 until 1949

In March 1941, the allied army retook both Somalia and West Somalia (Ogaden) for the period 1941—1949. Great Britain controlled most Somali areas except French Somaliland. This period of unity in the region had originally helped create a pan Somali identity that would become stronger during the independence struggle. The British encouraged the Somalis in the southern parts, to organise political parties. Ushering in, the establishment of the first political party of Somalia in 1943; the Somaili Youth Club which later on was renamed the Somali Youth League (SYL). In response another political party sprung up in the south; Hisbia Digel and Milifle (HDM) in 1947. The future of Somalia fell to the Allied Council of Foreign Ministers. At the time, the British were preferred because they offered promise of a better Somali future. Britain controlled all Somalia thus a chance to fulfill our dream of a 'Great Somalia'. I could not understand the reason why our leaders chose Italy, because Italy had colonised us and at the same time forced Somali people to enter in the Second World War. Many Somali soldiers died in the war. Therefore, we wanted nothing to do with Italy.

Our setback

There were many set back's for Somali people due to the fact that Somalis did not choose the British, these are:

We read in the history that there was a railway between Jowhar and

Mogadishu. Now I wonder where has the railway gone? Has it disappeared with the wind? It is evident that there is no railway in the map over leaf since 1914—1941.

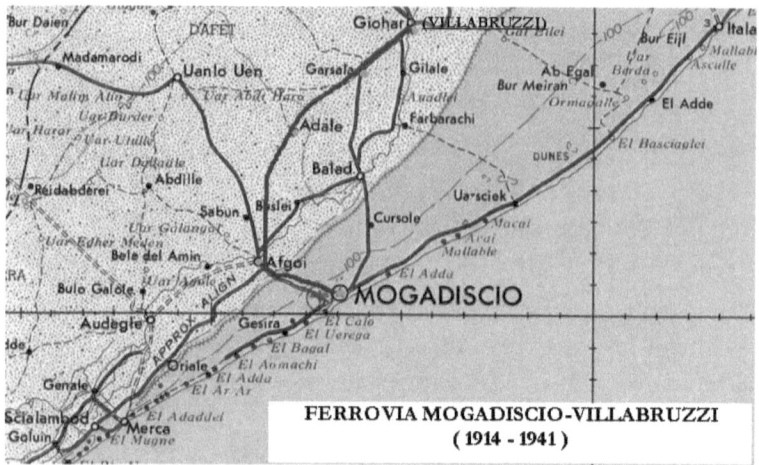

FERROVIA MOGADISCIO-VILLABRUZZI
(1914 - 1941)

Prince Luigi Amedeo, Duke of the Abruzzi, founder of Villaggio duca degli Abruzzi (Jowhar) the main agricultural colony in Italian Somalia "the result of our bad choice was that we lost our gracious people and lands."

West Somalia and the Northern Frontier District (NFD) were annexed to our neighbour countries, all this happened as a result of bad decisions.

The conditional return of Italian administration to southern Somalia gave the new trust territory several unique advantages compared with other African colonies. To the extent that Italy held the territory by a UN mandate. The trusteeship provision gave the Somalis the opportunity to gain experience in political education and self-government. These advantages did not retain British Somaliland, which was to be incorporated into the new Somali State. In the 1950's British colonial officials attempted, through various development efforts to further the process however the protectorate stagnated. The disparity between the two territories in economic development and political experience caused serious difficulties when it came time to integrate the two parts. The UN agreement established the Italian Trusteeship Administration (Aminitrazione Fiduciaria Italiana della Somalia - AFIS) to prepare southern Somalia for independence over a ten year period. Under the agreement, a UN Advisory Council (consisting of Egypt, the Philippines and Columbia) based in Mogadishu to observe the AFIS and report its progress to the UN Trusteeship council. The agreement required the new administration to develop the colony's political institutions, to expand the educational system, to improve the economic infrastructure, and to give the Somali people freedom of speech and the right to discuss political freedom. These political and civil guarantees did not make for smooth Italy—Somali relations. It was seen by the Italians as a source of nationalist sentiment and activity. The SYL distrusted the new administration, suspecting it of having a hidden colonial agenda. SYL fears were to increase violence when the AFIS took control, where they proceeded to jail some SYL members and fired others from their civil service posts.

The SYL responded with protests, civil disobedience and representations to the UN Advisory Council. The council intervened to arbitrate the disputes and to encourage the two sides to collaborate. The conflict simmered for three years, 1950-1953.

The Italian plan was to stimulate local agriculture, to improve the infrastructure and to expand educational facilities thus exports responded to this stimuli from 1954 to 1960. Despite improvement, an acute balance of payment deficit persisted and the administration had to rely on foreign grants and Italian subsidies to balance the budget. Development efforts in education were more successful between 1952 and 1957. Student enrollment at the elementary and secondary levels doubled. In 1957 there were 2,000 students receiving secondary, technical, and university education in Somalia. Scholarship progammes were provided from different countries such as China, Egypt and Italy. Another progam offered night school adult literacy instruction and provided further training to civil servants. However, these progams were severely handicapped by the absence of a standard script and a written national language;

Arabic, Italian and English served as the media of instruction in the various schools, this linguistic plurality created a Tower of Babel (international drama film well known).

Progress was made throughout 1950 in fostering political institution in accordance with a UN resolution in 1950. The Italians had established an advisory body known as the Territorial Council which took an active part in discussions of the proposed AFIS legislation composing thirty-five members. The council came to be dominated by representatives of political parties such as the SYL and HDM. Acting as a nascent parliament, the Territorial Council gained experience in procedural matters and also in legislative debates including the political, economic and social problems that would face future Somali governments. For its part the AFIS, by working closely with the council, won legitimacy in Somali eyes.

There were other forums, besides the Territorial Council, in which Somalis gained executive and legislative experience. These included the forty-eight member Municipal Council introduced in 1950, whose members dealt with urban planning, public services and after 1956, fiscal and budgetary matters. Rural councils handled tribal and local problems, such as conflicts over grazing and access to water and pasture lands. However, the effectiveness of the rural councils was undermined by the wandering of nomads as they searched for water wells and pastures, a circumstance that made stable political organizations difficult to sustain. Thus the UN Advisory Council's plans to use the rural councils as bridges to development turned out to be unsustainable. This situation enabled AFIS appointed district commissioners to become the focus of power and political action.

Territory wide elections were first held in southern Somalia in 1956. Although ten parties fielded candidates for representatives, to a new seventy-seat Legislative Assembly that was to replace the Territorial Council the SYL won forty-three seats, the SDM won thirteen seats with the remaining ten seats reserved for Indians, Arabs, and other non-Somali candidates.

Abdullah Lise Mohamud, the leader of the SYL became the first Prime Minister of a government composed of five ministerial posts, all held by Somalis. The new Assembly assumed responsibility for domestic affairs. However the governor as a representative of the Italian government, retained the 'power of absolute veto' as well as the authority to rule by emergency decree should the need arise. Moreover, until 1958 the AFIS continued to control important areas such as foreign relations, external finance, defence and public order.

The term of Abdullahi Ise's government was four years (1956—60) a trial period that enabled the nascent southern Somali administration to shape the terms under which it was to gain its independence. This period was the most stable in modern Somali politics. The government's outlook was modernist and the Somalis became convinced that Italy would not attempt to postpone independence. The franchise was extended to women in 1958 and nationalization at all levels of administration, from district commissioner to provincial governor proceeded quickly. Attempts were made to suppress clannishness and to raise the status of women and of groups holding low level occupations. The future promised hope with: the moral support of global anticolonial forces, the active backing of the UN and the goodwill of the Western powers, including Italy.

The southern Somali government's principal tasks were to increase economic self sufficiency and to find external sources of financial assistance that would replace the foreign support that Italy would withdraw after independence. Another major concern was to frame the constitution that would take effect once Somalia became independent. The writers of this document faced two sensitive issues: the form of government—either the federalist the version of (SDM) or unitary (SYL) the new nation would adopt and nationalist aspirations concerning Greater Somalia. The first issue was of great interest to the HDM, whose supporters were mainly cultivators from the well-watered region between the Shabeelle and Jubba rivers and who represented about 30% of the population. The HDM wanted a federal form of government. This preference derived from concerns about dominance by the SYL, which was supported by pastoral clans that accounted for 60% of the population. Not surprisingly the SYL advocated a unitary form of government, arguing that federalism would weaken the SYL to prevail.

The delicate issue of Greater Somalia, whose recreation would entail the indifference from Ethiopia and Kenya of Somali; inhabited areas, presented Somali leaders with a dilemma: they wanted peace with their neighbours but making claims on their territory was certain to provoke hostility. Led by Haaji Mahammad Husseen, the SYL radical wing wanted to include in the constitution an article calling for the unification of the Somali nation 'by all means necessary' ending the moderate majority, prevailed in modifying the wording to demand 'reunification of the dismembered nation by peaceful means'.

During the four year transition to independence conflicts over unresolved economic and political issues took the form of an intraparty power struggle within the dominant SYL rather than interparty competition. As a result party supporters banded into factions. Some segment of SYL accused Abdullahi Iise's government of being under Italian influence and another segment of SYL countered with a charge of clannishness. Hagi Mohamed Husseen's radical faction continued to charge Abdullahi Iise's government with being too close to the West and to Italy in particular and of doing little to realize the national goal of reconstituting a greater Somalia. Despite being at odds with Prime Minister Lise Husseen, who had headed the party in the early years, was again elected SYL president in July 1957. His agenda of looser ties with the West and closer relations with the Arab world clashed with the policies of Lise and Adan Abdullah Usmaan, the parliamentary leader who would become the first president of independent Somalia. Husseen angrily disapproved against 'reactionaries in government,' a thinly veiled reference to Lise and Osman. The latter two responded by expelling Husseen and his supporters from the SYL. Having lost the power struggle, Husseen created a militant new party, the Greater Somali League (GSL). Although Huseen's firebrand politics continued to worry the SYL leadership, he never managed to cut deeply into the party's constituency.

The SYL won the 1958 municipal elections in the Italian trust territory, in part because it had begun to succeed, in attracting important clan elements like Abdulqaadir Soppe who formerly had supported the HDM. Its growing appeal put the SYL in a commanding position going into the pre-independence election campaigns for the National Assembly of the Republic (a new body that replaced the two legislative assembly Italian Somali). The National Assembly had been enlarged to contain ninety seats for southern representatives and thirty-three for northern representatives. The HDM and the GSL accused the SYL of corruption with the election process deciding to boycott the elections and consequently, the SYL gained sixty seats and won the election and the government formed in 1959 was headed by the current Prime Minister Abdullah Lise Mohamud.

The SYL opened branches in the north and the SNL continued to expand its membership. This changed in 1954, when the last British liaison officers withdrew from the Reserved Areas—parts of the west of Somalia and the Haud in which the British had been given temporary administrative rights. This was in accordance with a 1942 military convention between Britain and the Ethiopian emperor. This move and Britain's agreement with Ethiopia, confirmed the latter's title deeds to the Haud, under the 1897 treaty that granted Ethiopia, full jurisdiction over the region. The British colonial administrators of the area were embarrassed by what they saw as Britain's betrayal of the trust put in them by the Somali clans who were to be protected against Ethiopian raids.

The Somalis responded with dismay to the ceding of the Haud to Ethiopia. A new party named the National United Front (NUF) supported by both the SNL and the SYL was rising under the leadership of a Somali civil servant, Michael Mariano, a prominent veteran of the SYL's formative years. The man selected to lead the nationalist visited London and the UN, seeking to have the Haud issue brought before the world community, in particular the International Court of Justice. Britain countered by laying a claim to all Somali territories - including the British and Italian Somaliland's.

Haile Selassie claimed this was a part of historical Ethiopian territory, seized by the European powers during a period of Ethiopian weakness. The Europeans were reluctant to press new territorial demands on Haile Selassie and did little to help the Somalis recover the Haud.

In 1956 political protests forced Britain to introduce representative government in its protectorate and to accept the eventual unification of British Somaliland with Southern Somalia. Accordingly, in 1957 a Legislative Council was established comprising six members appointed by the governor to represent the principal clan-families. The council was expanded the following year to consist of twelve elected members, two appointees and fifteen senior elders and notables, chosen from official members. The electoral procedure in the north followed that in the south, with elections in urban areas conducted by secret ballot and in the countryside by acclamation in clan assemblies. In 1960 the first elections contested along party lines, resulted in a victory for the SNL and its affiliate the USP. The two won between them, all but one, of the thirty-three seats in the new Legislative Assembly. The remaining seat was won by Machiel Mariano of the NUF's. This defeat was clearly attributable to his Christian affiliation, which his political opponents had used prominently as a campaign issue.

Following the election, Mahammad Ibrahim Igaal was chosen as prime minister to lead a four-man government. Popular demand compelled the leaders of the two territories to proceed with plans for immediate unification. The British government accepted the force of Somali nationalist public opinion and agreed to terminate its rule of Somaliland in 1960. In time, the protectorate would merge with the trust territory on the independence date, fixed by the UN commission. In July 1960, leaders of the two territories met in Mogadishu and agreed to form a unitary state with the elected president to be head of state. Full executive powers would be held by a prime minister who was answerable to an elected National Assembly of 123 members, representing the two territories.

Accordingly, British Somalia received its independence on June 26, 1960 thus uniting with the trust territory, to establish the Somali Republic on July 1, 1960. His Excellency Adan Abdulle Osman became president; he in turn appointed Shermaarke the first prime minister. Sherkmaarke formed a coalition government dominated by the SYL but supported by the two clan-based northern parties, the SNL and the USC. Usmaan's appointment as president was ratified a year later in a national referendum. (Paolo, 1999)

Chapter six

INDEPENDENCE AND UNIFICATION 1960

Prior to independence, a country should have a national Flag that is adopted by legislative council and it was important for the Somali people to know their National flag. To further this, His Excellency Mohamed Awale Liban had proposed that only Somali members should discuss the issue of their own Flag, even though there were foreign members in the legislative council such as Indians and Arabs. According to the legislative council's constitution, each new proposal had to be voted on by the legislative council members and Mr. Mohamed Awale Liban's proposal succeeded. The session was postponed and the next day commenced at 10:30am. However, when the chairman Mr. Sheik Omar opened the session, Mr. Liban requested permission of the chairman to give him a chance to speak. The chairman allowed this. Mr. Liban stood up in front of the legislative council members and stretched out in front of his chest, a blue Flag with a white star in the middle. Holding the flag open, some of the Somalis members applauded and cheered, while clapping for five minutes. The acting Somalian chairman made a short speech in which he mentioned the greatness and ability of Mr. Liban, whose talent had produced such a beautiful Flag in less than twenty-four hours. Mr. Mohamed Awale Liban said the blue colour stands for the UN who helped us to gain our dream of independence; the white means peace and prosperity; and the star is the five regions of Somali. The flag was adopted on October 12, 1954. From that day, Somalia had its National Flag.

Abdullahi Issa Mohamud was born in 1921 in the southern town of Afgoi thirty kilometres from Mogadishu. His father died a couple months after his birth; his mother subsequently moved the family to Mogadishu. Abdullahi Issa attended an Italian primary school in Mogadishu as well as the local Qur'anic school. When the Second World War broke out, he was still a student. At the age of sixteen Abdullahi was relocated to the port of Merca where he worked as a postal clerk, and later he returned to Mogadishu and obtained a position in the Department of Economic Affairs. When the British military occupied Somalia in 1940s' he was relieved of his duties and thus embarked on a business career. In the turmoil of the war year and at the age of thirty-eight Issa joined the Somali Youth League (SYL).

He was intelligent, largely self-educated, confident and determined. In 1948, he was appointed to the SYL's central committee and rose to the position of Secretary General.

He went to Paris and New York as a SYL delegate to proclaim the right of Somali people to independence. In 1956 he was appointed as the first prime Minister and he formed the first Somali government staying in this position as prime minister until 1959. After Independence (1 July 1960) he was appointed and moved to a new role that of foreign minister. In this capacity, he took part in many international conventions, in particular the United Nations General Assembly. After the revolution seized power in 1969, he was appointed as Somali Ambassador to Sweden in 1974 and he held this position until early 1983 when he resigned from public office, after a long and successful career in politics.

He spent his retirement years in Rome, Italy and died there in

Mach 1988 then his body was transported to Mogadishu for burial. At midnight of 1 July 1960, when the clock started to ring, the Somali nation was born and the national flag began to wave, in the sky over Mogadishu. It was a great night for Somali people after years of being colonized, from 1880 until 1960, almost eighty years.

On that day south Somalia and north Somalia united to form the Somali Republic, albeit within boundaries drawn up by Italy and Britain. A government was formed; His Excellency Aden Abdullah Osman became president of the Republic.

Aden Abdullah Osman was born 1908 in Belet Weyne; He was a member of the nationalist Somali Youth League (SYL) from 1954 to 1960. After Independence, he became the first president of Somalia and had a seven-year term as president. During his presidency, he worked tirelessly for peace and prosperity for the Somali people. He appointed Abdurashid Ali Shermerke as Prime Minister of Somalia on 12 July 1960 with a term till 14 June 1964. Next he appointed Abdirazaq Hagi Hussein as prime Minister of Somalia from 14 June 1964 to 15 July 1967. Abdirazaq Hagi Hussein was born on the 24 December 1924 in Galkayo and was of the Somali Youth League and he played an important role in the nation's early Civilian administration. The government of Abdirazaq was a test of democracy in the Somali Republic. He tried to steer the machine of the government in a new direction and strongly believed that Somalia's political and diplomatic future can be best served through the English language. He struggled to break that isolation and lead the Republic into political and diplomatic maturity. Many changes happened during his government which are not necessary to narrate. (The Dawn of the Somalia Nation— state 1960)

In the 1967 presidential election, Aden Abdullah Osman lost the election. Peacefully he handed power over to his successor President Abdurashid Ali Shermerke. Aden Abdullah Osman died June 8, 2007 in Nairobi, Kenya.

Abdirashid Ali Shermake was born on November 16th 1919 in Harardhere in the District of Hobyo but raised in Mogadishu; he attended Qur'anic school and completed his elementary education in 1936. He then embarked on a career as a trader and later as a civil servant in the Italian colonial administration. In 1943 he joined the Somali Youth League (SYL). He completed his secondary education in 1953 earning a scholarship to study at the prestigious Sapienza University of Roma, where he graduated in political science in 1958. On the 10th June 1967 he was elected as the president of republic of Somalia. He was assassinated on 15 Oct 1969 by one of his bodyguards. Somali people honour him and remember his famous speech during the war against Ethiopia in 1964. Dr Sharmarke said, "We join the elections and we are voting with our right hand and with our left hand we took the rifle to defend the country from Ethiopians, our enemy and my dream is to liberate Somalia from colonial power, Ogden, NFD and Djibouti".

Both Aden Abdullah Osman and Shermake were from the south and it was better to give one position to someone from the north, they would be able to come to Mogadishu without preconditions and in good faith. Somalia was one tribe without any differences so the North people were happy with the division of power. On July 20, 1961 and through a popular referendum, the people of Somalia ratified a new constitution, first drafted in 1960. In 1967, when Abdirashid Ali Shermake became president he appointed Mohamed Ibrahim Egal as Prime Minister. On October 15, 1969, while Shermarke was paying a visit to the northern town of Las Anode, President Abdirashid was shot dead by one of his bodyguards. His assassination was quickly followed by a military coup d'état. On October 21 1969, the Somali Army seized power in a bloodless manner. (Lewis, 1988)

Abdirazaq Hagi Hussein was born on the 24th December 1924 in Galkayo and was of the Somali Youth League playing an important role in the nation's early civilian administration. He was prime Minister of Somalia from 14 June 1964 to 15 July 1967. The government of Abdirazaq was a test democracy in the Somali Republic and tried to steer the machine of the government onto a new direction and strongly believed that Somalia's political and diplomatic future could be best served through the English language. He struggled to break that isolation and to lead the Republic into political and diplomatic maturity. As you may know, many changes happened during his government that are not necessary to narrate. (The Dawn of the Somalia Nation—state 1960)

He was Prime minister of Somalia, born on August 15 1928 in the north western town of Odweyne in Burco region, it was a part of the British Somaliland protectorate. Egal initially worked as an unofficial member of the former British Somaliland protectorate's Executive council and was the leader of Government Business in the Legislative Council. For five days in June 1960, he served as Prime Minister of the brief; present State of Somaliland, during its planned transition to union with, the Trust Territory of Somalia (the former Italian Somali) forming the Somali Republic. Following Somalia's independence on July 1, 1960, Egal became the first National Minister of Defence (1960 to 1962). In 1962, he left the government to form the opposition Somali National Congress and two years later he joined the Somali Youth League, the majority party in the government at that time.

In 1967, When Abdirashid Ali Shermarke became President of the Republic, he appointed his Excellency Mohamed Ibrahim as the Prime Minister.

Egal was on an official visit in Washington D.C., when President Abdirashid was assassinated on October 15, 1969. Immediately he returned to Mogadishu and participated in the President's funeral. After the coup d'état on (21 October 1969) led by Major General Mohamed Siad Barre, who created the Supreme Revolutionary Council (SRC)the SRC subsequently renamed the country the Somali Democratic Republic.

The SRC took the following steps:
- arrested members of the former civilian government.
- banned political parties.
- dissolved the parliament.
- abrogate the Supreme Court.

- and suspended the constitution.

Mohamed Hagi Ibrahim was among the politicians detained by the SRC for his prominent role in the nation's early government. He was eventually released and was appointed the Ambassador to India (1976 to 1978). When the Somali Government collapsed in 1991, north Somalia declared the region independent. Although Egal initially opposed their self-proclaimed succession, he was elected as president of the new Somaliland for two years.

During his occupancy as President of Somaliland, Egal managed to disarm local rebel groups, stabilized the north western Somaliland region's economy and established informal trade ties with foreign counties. He also introduced the Somaliland shilling, passport and flag. In Addition, Egal helped create the Somaliland army, one of the more effective armed forces in Somalia. Throughout his term as president of Somaliland region, Egal's dedication to the secessionist cause was doubted and challenge by hardliners, particularly within the Somali National movement (SNM) who believed that ultimately he still could reconcile with other political actors in the rest of Somalia. In one of his speeches he clearly declared that "Somalia will unite one day" and he continued with "we will talk to the southerners when they make their home clean and negotiate with them"

Mohamed Hagi Ibrahim died on May 3, 2002 in Pretoria, South Africa while undergoing surgery at a military hospital. He was returned to Somaliland for a state funeral, in accordance with his last wishes.

Mohamed Siad Barre was born in Shilavo, his parents died when he was ten years old and after receiving his primary education in the town of Luuq in southern Somalia, Barre moved to Mogadishu, the capital of Somalia to pursue his secondary education.

In 1940 He enrolled in the Italian colonial police as a Zaptie. He later joined the colonial police force during the British military administration of Somalia, rising to the highest possible rank.

In 1950, shortly after Italian became a UN Trustee in Somalia, he attended the Carabinieri police school in Italy for two years. Upon his return to Somalia, he remained with the military and eventually became Vice Commander of Somalia's Army when the country gained its independence in 1960. When he embarked on a revolution in 1969 he believed in a socialist government and a stronger sense of nationalism. Mohamed Barre was the president of the Somali Democratic Republic from 1969 to 1991. There are many reasons that caused the coup d'état in that year 1969 and I will now explain these:

Lack of the experience: Somali people were undergoing crucial times and in a phase of trial and error. This stage is well known in the history of any society. As the statesman and historian Winston Churchill said "Every nation's or group of nations has its own tale to tell. Knowledge of trial and struggles is necessary to all who would comprehend the problem, perils, challenges and opportunities which confront us today". On the other hand, Somalis did not understand the workings of a democracy and what it entailed in the political sphere, in which all eligible citizens have an equal say in the decisions that affect their lives. Democracy allows eligible citizens to participate equally—either directly or indirectly through elected representatives— in the development and making of decisions, encompassing political, social, economic and cultural conditions that enable the free will and equal practice of political self-determination. A democratic government contrasts the form of dictator government, anarchy or where power is held by a small number of individuals, as in an oligarchy. Democracy is focusing on opportunities for the people to control their leaders and to oust them without the need for a revolution and in Somalia we did not understand this system therefore, did not know how to apply these democratic methods.

Electoral fraud: electoral fraud is interference with the process of an election, affecting vote counts to bring about an election result, whether by increasing the vote share of the favoured candidate or depressing the vote share of the rival candidates. Such activities are morally unacceptable, illegal, outside the spirit of electoral law and in violation of the very principle of democracy. Thus doing so, is disrupting human beings free will. So, 1967 Somalia national election was fraudulent, the result was a coup d'état. It broke down the democracy and the establishment of military regime.

Nepotism: usually takes the form of employing relatives or appointing them in high office that they do not merit which replaces outsiders who may be better qualified. It has a negative impact on the whole society. In Somalia this harmful act was supported by ministers and by MP's making it very difficult to find employment freely before the revolution and then impossible if you were not supported by minister or MP. (Lewis, 1988)

Chapter seven

THE GOLDEN YEARS OF SOMALIA (1970 - 1977)

On 21st October 1969, the Somali military seized power in a bloodless coup and dissolved the National Assembly. They suspended the constitution and disbanded all political parties, set up National Security courts (NSC) and placed Major Gen. Mohamed Siad Barre as the head of the Supreme Revolutionary Council (SRC). Mohamed Siad Barre's main support outside the military came from urban intellectual and technocrats who wished to diminish the power of clan identification and establish Somalia as a modern nation. The protagonist of the coup had no real ideological plan; their driving force was to end tribalism, nepotism, corruption and misrule. SRC was the governing body during this regime. The revolution renamed Somalia to the Somali Democratic Republic. Shortly after the coup, the SRC defined its domestic policy in the first Charter of the Revolution and this charter also detailed the source of political power. Law one of the charter covered all the functions of the president, National Assembly, council of ministers (cabinet) and the courts. The SRC consisted of twenty-five members all of them military. There was the council of secretaries of State (CSS). The CSS was essentially the Cabinet responsible for the execution of the daily functions of government. The Revolution also nationalized manufacturing, agricultural trades and accelerated the development of infrastructure. This crash program was put in place to rapidly increase economic and social development. One of the main objectives of the program was also to establish a written standardized form of the Somali language. In 1974-5, when a long drought (abar dabadherti as they said Somalis) destroyed approximately 30% of Somalia's livestock and there was decreased agricultural output. Many Somalia were faced with famine and at the same time the government incurred a sharp rise in debt as a result of the infrastructure spending.

In 1976, the SRC convened the Somali Revolutionary Socialist Party (SRSP) to transform the SRC into a legitimate political body with a Supreme Revolution Council which would act as its new central committee. This Supreme council was to consist of ninety-three members of whom ninety would be from the SRC with additional seats being held by civilian advisors, heads of ministers and public figures. A Council of Ministers were to replace the CSS and his five member council was to act as executive power (politburo) their names are:

General Mohamed Siyad Bare
Secretary General of the SRSP and Chairman of the Council Ministers

Brig. General Mohamed Ali Samatar
First vice president and minister of defence

Brig. General Hussein Kulmiye Afrah
Second vice president

Coronel Ismail Ali Abucar
Third vice president, who later replaced Ahmed Mohamud Farah when xcIsmail Ali Abucar was jailed

Brig. General Ahmed Suleiman Abdulla
The Commander of Somalia National Security (SNS)

Military officers replaced civilian district and regional officials. Meanwhile, civil servants attended reorientation courses that combined professional training with political indoctrination. Those found to be incompetent or politically unreliable were fired and amass dismissal of civil servants happened in 1974, dictated in part by economic pressures.

The legal system functioned after the coup, subject to modification. In 1970 the National Security Courts (NSC) special tribunal was set up as the judicial arm of the SRC. Using a military attorney as prosecutor, the courts operated outside the ordinary legal system as watchdogs against activities considered to be counter revolutionary. The national security court dealt with the case of President Abdirashid Ali Shermaarke's assassination and a charge of corruption leveled by the SRC against members of the civil regime. The NSC subsequently heard cases with and without political content. A uniform civil code introduced in 1973 replaced predecessor laws inherited from the Italians and British and also imposed restrictions on the activities of Sharia courts.

The SRC intended to destroy the influence of the traditional clan assemblies and in the words of the government, to bring government closer to the people. Local councils composed of military administrators and representatives appointed by the SRC were established under the Ministry of Interior at the regional, district and village levels to advise the government on local conditions and to expedite its directives.

The SRC took its toughest political stance in the campaign to break down the solidarity of the lineage groups. Tribalism was condemned as the most serious impediment to national unity. SRC denounced tribalism in a wider context as a 'disease', obstructing development not only in Somalia, but also throughout the Third World. The Democratic government had paid a stipend and was replaced by reliable local dignitaries known as 'peacekeepers' (nabod Doon), appointed by Mogadishu to represent government interests. Community identification rather than lineage affiliation was forcefully advocated at orientation centres set up in every district as local political and social activities. In order to increase production and control over the nomads, the government resettled 140 000 nomadic pastoralists in farming communities and in coastal towns, where the former herders were encouraged to engage in agriculture and fishing.

In many instances, real improvement in the living conditions of resettled nomads was evident, but despite government efforts to eliminate it, clan consciousness as well as desire to return to the nomadic life persisted. Concurrent SRC attempts to improve the status of Somali women, and promulgated the family law that equaled the right of women to the same rights of man in heritage. There is a version in Qur'an in Surat Al Nisaa saying that "Allah instructs you concerning your children: for the male, what is equal to the share of two females". This position of the revolution was very a serious one because it was against the principal of the Islamic religion. As the result of efforts by the socialist regime to improve opportunities for women, Somali women have more freedom to become educated, to work and to travel than do most other Muslim women. Before the 1969 revolution, 20% of primary school students were girls; in 1979 the figure approached 40%.

The achievements of the revolution (Positives)

It is indisputable that the revolution achieved many goals after the 1969—1977 period, the country was in decline. Achievements are as follows:

The revolution wrote the Somali language, which civil government could not fulfill. There was conflict between two ideas; one demanded that it must be written in Arabic words (the other for it to be written in Latin). When the SRC examined both ideas, they saw that it is better to write it in Latin, because it was easy to find the means to fulfill projects.

The second step was to promote this new language so as to spread it all over the country. Previously there was chaos in public offices because Italian, English and even Chains were used.

The preeminent scholar of history explained, "The new regime provided community health programs, rural education and a literacy campaign and encouraged local communities to build schools, hospitals and dispensaries. Cooperatives and tree planting was encouraged and the Roman script was adapted for the Somali Language Christian Parent.

A program of self-reliance, in order to develop the country was introduced. I remember that after mid-day all the employees had to leave the offices in order to participate in the collective work, which was running in different districts in Mogadishu, school buildings, hospital buildings and roads, etc. Nobody could sleep in the afternoon when they had finished work. Everyone had to contribute to the National effort and it was a wonderful idea and projects were fulfilled in this way.

When Somalia was hit by drought in 1974—5 attention was given the settlement of 140,000 Somali families at river banks, where they trained to cultivate the land and to develop their lives from nomads to that of famers. This project was achieved with Soviet help.

The project called bacad cellin means to push back the sand from the agricultural areas in (Shalanbood) near Merca zone.

Politically, Somalia had joined the Arab League in 1974 which allowed Somalia to be a member in regional organizations such as OAU, OIC and Arab League.

As always both positive and negative aspects exist. Now I will talk about its negatives.

In my opinion the Revolution's the greatest mistakes are as follows

The first great mistake the Revolution committed was when it gave equality between men and female in regard of heritage. This is totally against the version in Qur'an. God judged it and so no one can tamper or change Surah Al—Nisa number (11), which says as follows:

Allah instructs you concerning your children: for the male, what is equal to the share of two females. But if there are [only] daughters, two or more, they are to receive two thirds of one's estate. And if there is only one, for her is half. And for one's parents, to each one of them is a sixth of his estate if he left children. But if he had no children and the parents [alone] inherit from him, then for his mother is one third. And if he had brothers [or sisters], for his mother is a sixth, after any bequest he [may have] made or debt. The parents or children, you know not which of them are nearest to you in benefit. These shares are an obligation, imposed by Allah. Indeed, Allah is ever knowing and wise. Therefore, this was a great trespass for Islamic society and for Somalia people. There are other verses that explained in Surah Al Imran Number 7, it said as follows; It is He Who has sent down to you (Muhammad SAW) the Book (this Qur'ân). In it are Verses that are very clear and the foundations of the Book [and those are the Verses of Al-Ahkâm (commandments), Al-Farâ'id (obligatory duties) and Al-Hudud (legal laws for the punishment of thieves and adulterers)]; and others not entirely clear. So as for those in whose hearts there is a deviation (from the truth) they follow that which is not entirely clear thereof, seeking Al-Fitnah (polytheism and trials) and seeking for the hidden meanings. But none knows its hidden meanings, save Allah. And those who are firmly grounded in the knowledge say: "We believe in it; the whole of it (clear and unclear Verses) are from our Lord." And none receive admonition except men of understanding. (Tafsir At-Tabarî).

Thus Revolution made its ideology a scientific socialism, knowing that the Somali people believed in the Islamic religion. At this point I do not know if the people who commanded the revolution were aware what of the significance of scientific socialism, as it is against all of our values and religions. Therefore, it was a mistake to demand it in Islamic society.

Somali foreign Policy

The Somali Foreign Ministry was established after Somalia became independent in 1960 to articulate Somalia's Foreign policy and international cooperation. For a long time, Somalia pursued a Foreign policy based on fundamental principles of promotion of peaceful co-existence, respect for sovereignty and territorial integrity of other states and preservation of national security, peaceful settlement of disputes, non- interference in the internal affairs of other states, non-alignment, national interest and adherence to the Charters of United Nations and African Union. But Somalia was always determined to achieve unification of all Somali territories (west Somalia and Northern Frontier District).

Therefore, Abdirashi Sharmerke, who was prime Minister from 1960 until 1964, was ousted from his position when he went to visit Italy with a request for arming Somali's new nascent army. Italy rejected the proposal. Sharmake promptly decided to go to the Soviet Union without consulting the president and parliament so he alone shifted Somalia from western bloc to eastern bloc, in order to arm the Somali military and or that reason Somalia had forty Embassies throughout the world, in order to promote its policy.

The Somali Government was not looking at the condition of the country's economy, only concerned with the unification of Somalia.

Somalia now had to rethink and reengineer its foreign policy and redesign a new strategy. It is time to consider social affairs such as health, education and human wellbeing.

Ogaden War (West Somalia)

Winston Churchill Said "The statesman who yields to war fever must realize that once the signal is given, he is no longer the master of policy but the slave of unforeseeable and uncontrollable events".

In July 1977, the Ogaden war broke out after the Somali government sought to incorporate the predominantly west Somali inhabited region into a Pan-Somali (Greater Somalia). In the first week of the conflict, the Somali armed forces seized the southern and central parts of West Somali. I preferred to call it west Somali instead of Ogden, because that is exclusive instead of inclusive. For most of the war, the Somali army scored continuous victories over the Ethiopian army.

By September 1977, Somalia controlled 90% of West Somalia and captured strategic cities such as Jigjigs and put heavy pressure on Dire Dawa, threatening the train route, which linked Hara and Djibouti. Then a massive unprecedented Soviet intervention consisting of 20 000 Cuban forces and several thousand Soviet experts came to the aid of Ethiopia's communist Derg regime. By 1978, the Somali troops were pushed out of the West Somalia.

The Ogaden War was a conventional conflict between Somalia and Ethiopia (1877 and 1878) over the Ogden region. Fighting erupted as Somalia sought to exploit a temporary shift in the regional balance of power in their favour to occupy the Ogden region, which was claimed to be part of Greater Somalia. In a notable illustration of the nature of Cold War alliances, the Soviet Union switched from supplying aid to Somalia to that of supporting Ethiopia, which had previously been backed by the United States, prompting the U.S. to start supporting Somalia. The war ended when Somali forces retreated back across the border and a truce was declared.

Origins of the war: While the cause of the conflict was the desire of the Somali government to incorporate the Somali-inhabited region of Ethiopia into a Greater Somalia, it is unlikely Barre would have ordered the invasion if circumstances had not turned in his favour. Ethiopia had historically dominated the region. By the beginning of the war, the Somali National Army (SNA) was only 35 000 men strong and was vastly outnumbered by the Ethiopian forces. However, throughout the 1970s, Somalia was the recipient of large amounts of Soviet military aid. The SNA had three times the tank force of Ethiopia, as well as a larger air force.

As Somalia gained military strength, Ethiopia grew weaker. In September 1974, Emperor Hailey Selassie had been overthrown by the Derg (the military council) marking a period of turmoil. The Derg quickly fell into internal conflict to determine who would have primacy. Meanwhile, various separatist movements developed throughout the country with the regional balance of power now in favour of Somalia.

A sign that order had been restored among the Derg, was the announcement of Mengistu Hailey Mariam as head of state on 11 February 1977. However, the country remained in chaos while the military attempted to suppress its civilian opponents. Despite the violence, the Soviet Union who had been closely observing developments, came to believe that Ethiopia was developing into a genuine Marxist-Leninist state and that it was in the Soviet interests to aid the new regime. Thus they secretly approached Mengistu with offers of aid that which he accepted.

In June 1977, Mengistu accused Somalia of infiltrating into the Ogden to fight alongside the Western Somali Liberation front (WSLF). Despite considerable evidence to the contrary, Barre insisted that no such thing was occurring.

The U.S.S.R. found itself supplying both sides of a war and attempted to mediate a ceasefire. When their efforts failed, the Soviets abandoned Somalia. All aid to Siyad Barre's regime was halted, while arms shipments to Ethiopia were increased. Soviet military advisors flooded into the country armed with 15 000 Cuban combat troops. Other Communist countries offered assistance: the People's Democratic Republic of Yemen offered military assistance and North Korea helped train a 'People's Militia'. As the scale of Communist assistance became clear in November 1977, Somalia broke diplomatic relations with the U.S.S.R. and Cuba and expelled all Soviet citizens from the country.

The greatest single victory of the SNA—WSLF was a second attack on Jigjig in mid—September, in which the Ethiopian troops mutinied and withdrew from the town. The local defenders were no match for the assaulting Somalis and the Ethiopian military was forced to withdraw past the strategic strongpoint of the Marda Pass, halfway between Jijiga and Harar. By September Ethiopia was forced to admit that it controlled only about 10% of the Ogden and that the Ethiopian defenders had been pushed back into the non-Somali areas of Harerge, Bale and Sidamo. Nevertheless, the Somalis were unable to press their advantage because of the high level of erosion among its tank battalions, constant Ethiopian air attacks on their supply lines and the onset of the rainy season which made the dirt roads unusable. The SNA ordered the retreat back into Somalia on 9 March 1978. The last significant Somali unit left Ethiopia on 15 March 1978, marking the end of the war.

From October 1977 until January 1978, the SNA—WSLF forces attempted to capture Harar, where 40 000 Ethiopians backed by Soviet-supplied artillery and amour had regrouped with 1 500 Soviet advisors and 11 000 Cuban soldiers. Though it reached the city border by November, the Somali force was too exhausted to take the city and eventually forced to retreat outside and await an Ethiopian counterattack.

The expected Ethiopian—Cuban attack occurred in early February. However, it was accompanied by a second attack that the Somalis were not expecting - a combined Ethiopian and Cuban force crossed northeast into the highlands between Jijiga and the border with Somalia by passing the SNA-WSLF force defending the Marda Pass. The attackers were thus able to assault from two directions, allowing the re-capturing of Jijiga in only two days. The Somali defence collapsed and every major Ethiopian town was recaptured in the following weeks.

Somalia was forced to seek allies elsewhere. All in all, Somalia's initial friendship with the Soviet Union had enabled them to build the largest army in Africa. This war weakened the Somali military as well as it weakened the Somalia government.

After that the Somalia society split with the army and the economy ruined. The result of this was that opposition movements were established, such as: SSDF, SNM, USC, SPM. The security situation was out of control for days on end as various weapons fell in the hands of people and chaos returned to Somalia causing the collapse of Somali Government.

The Establishment of IGDD in January 1986

The east Africa states established Inter Governmental Authority Drought and Development in Djibouti, these states included Somalia, Ethiopia, Sudan, Uganda Kenya and Djibouti. For this reason, His Excellency Mengistu was in Djibouti. Our delegation was composed of His Excellency President Mohamed Siad Barre, Mohamed Ali Hamud Minister of State for foreign Affairs and Ahmed Mohamed Qaybe, permanent secretary of Foreign Affairs. His Excellency Mohamed Siad Barre called us, as foreign personnel myself and Ahmed Mohamed (Qaybe) and asked us to prepare points to put in front of President Mengistu. This was because we wanted to promote our relationship. So Ahmed and I brainstormed the issue and set out the following points:

- In order, to advance our relationship we must stop the propaganda between us.

- To disengage our troops on the border from 15km on both sides.
- To reinstate the Diplomatic relation between the two countries.
- To exchange prisoners.

We will discuss the other matters once the above points are accepted by the President Mengistu.

The Next day His Excellency Mohamed Said Barre and his delegation met with President Mengistu we outlined the four points, then he surprised us saying "I had no mandate to sign this agreement until I consult with my people in Addis".

President Barre answered by saying in a mocking way, "I am a dictator and I do not consult anybody you are the same, so let us sign the agreement". President Mengistu smiled and said His Excellency I will send you my foreign minister as soon as possible after my return to Addis". He fulfilled his promise and sent to Mogadishu His Excellency Berhanu Bayih, Minister of Foreign Affairs of Ethiopia to Mogadishu. At that time I was overseas and so instead of me, he was welcomed by His Excellency Ahmed Mohamud Farah who was at that time political advisor to the Presidency and they both signed the agreement. The next time the two presidents met was in 1987 (Refer to the frank discussion below)

Frank Dialogue between the two presidents

In 1987, President Mohamed Siyad Barre participated at the African Organization Union (OAU). It was the first time president Mohamed Siyad Barre had participated at the OAU summit since 1977 when the war broke out between Somalia and Ethiopia. Our delegation consisted of the President, I as acting Foreign Minister at that time and some high ranking officials. While the meeting of the summit was underway, his Excellency Berhanu Bayih (Ethiopian minister of foreign affairs) contacted us saying that the president Mengistu requested us to remain for two days after the end of a summit in order to continue our talk.

We accepted the request and stayed when the summit ended his Excellency president Mengistu came to us and we all left Addis.

I think the place we travelled to Sodare arriving at mid-day, taking our lunch and resting.

At four o'clock we met in a meeting room, where we exchanged greetings. Mr. Mengistu took the floor and he told us that he had issued the order for his people on the border, telling them that Somalia and Ethiopia had agreed to end subversive activities and hostile propaganda against each other. Therefore, the SNM movement must know that they have two options; to withdraw their troops inside Ethiopia or we would ask president Syad to give them pardon.

When the Ethiopian people told the SNM that there was peace between the two countries, one officer addressed the Somalian's and said "I hope that you inform your people in the area". After that, he started to talk about other important issues saying that this evening, we will talk with frankness. Let me tell you Somalis you are dreaming Harar and awash. We are as Ethiopia; we are dreaming that our border is near Balcad. Therefore let us be realistic and we can finish this issue between us? We are free people let us discuss it openly.

It was His Excellency Mohamed Siyad's turn to take the floor and speak. First of all he thanked Mr. Mengistu for his good words and continued with; the problem between us is comes from you side, not from the Somalia side and if you are ready to solve the problem then we are ready also but I think you are not ready yet. Thus the meeting ended in a congenial manner and we agreed to meet the next day at ten o'clock. When we had left the meeting I followed His Excellency President Mohamed Siad Barre to his room, where I said to him, "Excellency you had heard what President Mengistu said, tomorrow when we meet, what will be our position? Suggesting we need some experts who know the area and typographic people". He interrupted me saying "that they are not going to write in the history Mohamed Siad Barre gave up one inch of Somali and therefore I am not going to stand in the way of the future generation, let them fulfill what we could not achieved".

There is an Italian proverb that says "L' umo propone Il Dio Dispose" (Humans make plans but only What God wants happens in the end). That night, May 27 1988, SNM troops captured the city Burco and then part of Hargeysa on May 31 and I heard this on an early morning newscast from the BBC London. I rushed to the president's room and I found that he had been up all night on the direct line to Mogadishu (He was already aware of the matter). We tried to locate a helicopter for General Mohamed Said Morgan, who was with us the Commander of (SNA) Governor of Hargeysa. Eventually, a Helicopter was ordered it to fly to Burco and Hargeysa. At the same time, the delegation retuned to Mogadishu. Therefore, the dialogue ended without a result.

Chapter eight

SOMALI LOST DIGNITY (AFTER GOVERNMENT COLLUSION IN 1991)

After Mohamed Siad Barre fled the country, the USC established an interim provisional government headed by the provisional President Ali Madi Mohammed. In September 1991, Somalia was effectively under the control of many rival clans and sub clans. Somalia comprised of roughly 7.5 million people and the establishment of the government proved to be extremely difficult so at this time Somalia remained a lawless nation.

Somali Patriotic Movement (SPM) joined forces to fight against Mohamed Said Barre's government. In 1990 as Mohamed Siad Barre began to lose control of the country, the local political and business figures came together to sign the Mogadishu Manifesto, calling for Barre's resignation. Somalia has not had a central government since President Siyad Barre fled in 1991, leaving the country to the mercy of its numerous warring factions and under clan or Islamic Shari'ah law rule's. That was because of the continuing unrest in south Somalia. The stability in Somaliland and Puntland were relatively better than south Somalia in which domination by clan militias, banditry and looting made the free movement of people, goods and services nearly impossible. At the Somali Peace conference held in Djibouti from May to August 2000, a Transitional National Assembly was established under a plan sponsored by Djibouti President Ismail Omar Gelle and endorsed by the United Nations and the Organization of African Unity. The National congress, which was held in Djibouti elected Mr. Abdulqassin Salad Hassan as President of Somalia. Several neighbouring countries of Somalia have recognized Hassan's Transitional National Government and the UN have given it de facto recognition since President Salad Hassan participated in the General Assembly in September 2000. The authority of Hassan's government had not been established throughout the country.

Somalia did try to establish a formal government many times:
- The interim government headed by His Excellency Ali Mahdi Mohamed from 1991—1993.
- TNF headed by His Excellency Abdulqasim Salad Hassan from 2000—2004.
- TFG lead by HIS Excellency Abdullahi Yusuf Ahmed from 2004—2008.
- Headed by His Excellency Sharif Ahmed Sheikh from 2009—2012.
- The first time Somalia gained international recognition and passed through the transitional period. This time the Somali government was led by His Excellency Hassan Sheikh Mohamud. We had high hopes for him to be successful rescue of the Somali people from its long years of chaos and to put an end, to violation of human rights and deaths due to armed conflict.

When you compare and reflect what you had yesterday, with what you have today the comparison is very bad. The memories of 1970 to 1977 were positive, the world admired Somalia's achievements and the African nations looked to Somalia as a role model.

We were proud of our accomplishments, had confidence in our future and there were no disputes between us, we were at the pinnacle of success. Suddenly things happened and we changed! If we knew what was to transpire we would have done things differently. Are we regretful? Have we become a bad example to the world? Can we conclude that we had lost our dignity? Now the question is; how can we save what can be saved?

Before 26 January 1991, the Somali people and its leaders were respected throughout the world. They held honourable status throughout the world both as officials and unique courageous forward thinking individuals. After the time (as just mentioned above) everything reversed, the people who were yesterday respected and honoured became disrespected and disgraced. The Somali people scattered all over the world as refugees or asylum seekers. Those who became refuges in European countries faced a cultural clash exacerbated by language differences. The young people at schools faced the same destiny, failed their studies and life became a hopeless struggle without options. Those who remained in Somalia have carried guns killing the people in the streets, looting and turning to drugs. As a result, Somalia has lost everything, internally and externally. Some Somalis died in the sea, while they ran from the fight, which was going in their country.

Somalia has suffered from a most severe civil war, drought and famine over the last twenty-one years. This resulted in the deaths of tens of thousands of people and endangered the lives of 750 000 more Somalis. This crisis tested the notion of civilization and our modern values. It reveals, once again, that it is a basic human obligation to pursue international cooperation and solidarity to provide support for those suffering from natural and man-made disasters.

We cannot ignore the fact that in addition to the drought, the international community's decision to abandon Somalia to its own fate is also an underlying factor furthering this drama. Twenty-one years of political and social instability, lawlessness and chaos have added enormously to the problems in Somalia. No person with common sense and a conscience can remain indifferent to such a drama, irrespective of where it is. The United Nations and other countries in 1992 offered urgent intervention. As responsible members of the international community they should have contributed to the alleviation of the Somali people's distress. However, the establishment of lasting peace and stability would have only been possible through long-term coordinated efforts. As this did not happen they failed to restore peace and stability in Somalia. I think their main task was only humanitarian. As a result they failed to restore peace, stability, to rebuild the country again and to support the Somalia people until they were able to stand on their feet, and form a new government.

Recently in 2011, Turkey mobilized a massive campaign to end the suffering for Somali people. We consider this solidarity a humanitarian obligation toward the people of Somalia. There were many other countries that Somalia had a closer relationship with but they have not helped the way Turkey has. Many of our institutions, NGO's and people of all ages, have made an extraordinary effort to alleviate the suffering of women and children in Somalia. We are proud of the sensitivity and cooperation displayed by the Turkish people during the holy month of Ramadan. In the last month alone, approximately $280 million worth of donations for Somalia were collected in Turkey. The Turkish people's generosity has served as an example to other donor countries as well as the international community, offering hope for the resolution of the crisis in Somalia. I am not saying that the Turkish government and its people only helped the Somali people; there are many governments who helped the Somali people from 1992, such as the United States of America, the UN and other countries and we never forgot what they did for the Somali people in 1992. But it was not enough; we needed to re-establish the Somali government so as to resolve our own problems. The Turkish government has also moved decisively to help alleviate this humanitarian crisis. Turkey took the initiative to hold an emergency meeting of the executive committee of the Organization of Islamic Cooperation (OIC) at the ministerial level on Aug 17th 2011. At this meeting, which was attended by the president of Somalia and high-level representatives from forty member countries of the OIC, $350 million was committed to help relieve the famine in Somalia and the participants agreed to increase this amount to half a billion dollars. The Turkish Red Crescent is also standing shoulder to shoulder with international aid organizations and is working to meet the needs of those in all the camps in the Mogadishu region. Turkey has decided to launch a major humanitarian effort to return normality to Mogadishu and end this tragedy. The Turkish spokesman of humanitarian organization in Mogadishu in 2011 stated "We are preparing to provide assistance in the fields of health, education and transportation. We will inaugurate a 400-bed hospital, provide garbage trucks for the streets of Mogadishu, build a waste—disposal facility to burn the accumulated garbage in the streets, pave the road between Mogadishu's airport and the city centre, renovate the parliament and other government buildings"

Why is Somalia's instability endless?

Regardless of the recent issues of this never- ending Somalia tragedy, some key facts should be called, in any rapid attempt to understand what's behind this?

The Somalis do not understand what good citizenship is, as their loyalty to their clan is greater than to their nation. This is the cause or the origin of problem.

The continuing interference of foreign powers in Somalia affairs.

The colonial legacy that disintegrated the Somali country.

The consequent increasing strength of the warlords armed and backed by foreign powers and encouraged by Washington's so-called war on terrorism.

The imposed confusion of too many businessmen trafficking in weapons, drugs, illegal fishing, and toxic, radioactive materials dumping and worse - human trafficking.

Somali people are scattering all over the world, some of them dying in the sea, others in the refugee camps and others as displaced people.

Chapter nine

SELF-DESTRUCTION AND LAWLESS STATE

As discussed in previous chapters Somalia's self destruction and the collapse of the government resulted in anarchy.

Population Death Rate

As reported by Care Australia between April 1992 and February 1993, based on specific results, mortality rates (per 10 000 per day) varied by survey site, ranging from 1.9 deaths per day in Jowhar and 2.9 per day in Merca/Qorioley to 11.8 per day in Bardera and 12.5 in Mogadishu. 11% of the population in Afgoi had died, that is according to surveys among surviving family members.

In most developing countries, the expected mortality of 10 000 per day for the general population is 0.5 (or approximately 2% of the total population died per year in the case of Somalia). Thus, the observed mortality rates during 1992 reflect an excess mortality ranging from 3.8 to 25 times the expected rate for a developing country.

Similarly, the percentage of the surveyed population, that died during the recall period (March 1992 to late 1992) ranged from 6% in Jowhar to 36% in the Marin camp in Mogadishu.

CARE Australia reports a total average mortality rate in the southwest Bay region of 2 people dying per family (mean family size of 8) giving a 25% crude mortality rate for the emergency period (April 1992 to February 1993). In a similar survey in Bur Hakaba, World Vision reported an 18% death rate during this period. It was reported that 39% of the population died in displaced camps around Baidoa. Among children younger than five years of age, the mortality rates were higher than that of the general population, with rates ranging from 3.2 per day in Mogadishu and 3.8 per day in Jowhar to 19.8 in Hoddur and 22.7 in Bardera. The expected mortality rate per 10,000 per day for children younger than five years of age in developing countries is 2. Thus, the observed mortality rates during 1992 reflect an excessive mortality ranging from 1.6 to 11 times the expected rate. The portion of the surveyed populations who died during the period ranged from 12% of children younger than five years of age. These children would be expected to die within an eight month period based on the daily mortality rate among developing countries.

Those surveys which separately examined mortality of displaced and non-displaced individuals consistently found that mortality rates were higher among the displaced. The highest mortality rates were generally observed among displaced persons residing in camps rather than towns and for displaced children residing in camps. Taking the highest displaced mortality rate (town or camp) from each survey, the mortality rate ranged from 4.6 to 16.8. Dislocation in itself was the most dramatic risk factor. The excess mortality relative to non-displaced people ranged from 1.5 to 3.7, with a midpoint of a two-fold excess mortality relative to non-displaced groups.

For displaced children under five years of age residing in camps, the mortality rate per 10, 000 per day ranged from 6.6 in Merca/Qorioley to 32.0 in Baidoa, rates that are 3.3 to 16 times the normal expected background rate of two deaths per 10, 000 per day. Among the four studies that compared displaced rates to non-displaced rates, the relative risk of excess of mortality among displaced children ranged from 1.3 to 2.1 with a midpoint value of a twofold excess above non-displaced rates.

The famine was typical, in that most of the lives lost were among the young: 47% of all deaths were under eight year of age. On the other hand, the proportion of all deaths suffered by the very young is usually higher. So, as a multiple of baseline conditions, the increase in death rates was proportionally more for adults. The famine in certain areas was so extreme that adults suffered severe malnutrition on a scale that is rare. Unlike famine victims in other parts of the world, these adults had too little body fat or protein to carry them through a prolonged period of deprivation. (Sage, 2005)

Minimum and Maximum Deaths

International observers witnessed and verified through surveys the levels of deaths in major population centres (principally during 1992). Based on their reports; a conservative estimate would put the number of deaths in Baidoa at least 20,000, 10,000 in Bardera, 10,000 in Mogadishu, 10,000 in Kismayo, 7,000 in Jowhar, 2,000 Afgoi, 5,000 in the Jilib area of the lower Juba and 5,000 in centres along the coast south of Mogadishu (e.g. Merca and riverside centres such as Quoreiley). Therefore if no excessive death occurred outside of the major populated centres, which we know not to be true, a minimum estimate would be that at least 70,000 people died due to the famine in 1992/1993.Mohamed Sahnoun, the representative of Secretary General of UN reported when he arrived in Somalia (that 300,000 had died from hunger by March 1992).Similarly, the percentage as surveyed that died during the recall period (from March 1992 to late 1992) ranged from 6% in Jowhar to 36% in the Marin camp in Mogadishu.

An Arabic proverb says "If the fire gets nothing to eat, it eats itself". Sadly, Somalia ate itself.

In conclusion

There are statistics that showed that between 1992—1993 one half (1.5) of all Somali children under five years died and between April 1992 and mid 1993, an estimated 250 000 to 300 000 Somalis died from the fighting in Mogadishu. These people died whilst in the face of the supposed restored hope in 1992. I am sure that you agree that these were senseless deaths of our people, they died in unknown places, in the sea or in the desert.

Somali Refugees in Neighbouring Countries: 2011

HOST COUNTRY	TOTAL NUMBER OF SOMALI REFUGEES
Kenya	520,230
Uganda	22,146
Ethiopia	181,271
Djibouti	18,748
Yemen	196,917
Eritrea	3,865
Total	943,177

Chapter ten

THE KUWAIT CRISIS

The Arab league emergency meeting in Cairo, which convened on 30 and 31 August 1990 as called by President Mubarak, deepened inter-Arab divisions in an unprecedented manner. The Egyptian president and Golf states sought concrete steps from the summit. These steps were as follows:

They wanted urgent action taken by Arab government's armed forces to support the region with peacekeeping. The Gulf States made a request to dispatch Arab forces to Kuwait to help them defend their territories 'against foreign aggression'.

The summit wanted the most tangible expression possible of Arab solidarity with the Saudi Arabia against the perceived Iraqi threat to its country. Therefore, the forces must be Arab peacekeeping,

To legitimize the above acts, there was an endorsement of Saudi Arabia's invitation to American forces to enter the Kingdom land to assist with its defence and Saudi Arabia's 'right of legitimate defence'. That means the request for foreign forces to be stationed in Saudi Arabia. This right was anchored in the Arab League's joint Defence Pact of 1950, Article 51 of the UN Charter and Security Council Resolution 661 adopted four days earlier. The summit started early morning, about 10 am, and continued all the day until 5 pm. The chairman tried to form a special committee to be sent to Baghdad to talk with Saddam. But the summit did not agree on the matter due to a controversy between member states.

There were two blocks; one tried to solve the problem and the other did not. What were the pros and cons? We didn't know until the chairman took votes. At that time, this seemed to be the destiny of the unity of the Arab League and it was very difficult to take a decision to support one side against the other. At that crucial moment, the chairman made a decision to vote on this dangerous issue.

The result of vote was as followed

Twelve states favoured resolution 195 were: Egypt, six GCC states, Syria, Lebanon, Morocco, Somalia and Djibouti. The 195 solution was taken before by the Arab League council of ministers on 10 August 1990. The other Arab States divided in different directions, some were absent such as Algeria, Yemen, Lybia and PLO abstained. Jordan, Sudan and Mauritania expressed their reservation. Tunisia did not attend the meeting because they had already expressed their positions by not attending and of course Iraq stayed away. However Iraq did not have the right to vote. This group sought to disrupt the summit by any means particularly President Ali Abdullah Salah, his colleagues and Yasir Arafat. But the dedication of the chairman did not allow them to do so.

The position of the Somali delegation

The President Hosni Mubarak called an emergency meeting in Cairo within twenty-four hours. At that time I was in Libya intending to deliver special letter from President Mohamed Siad Barre to the leader of Libya Mu'ammar Al Qadhafi. Then before I met with Qadhafi, he left for Cairo in order to participate in the Summit. I wondered whether I should return home or wait for him then the telephone in my room rang. Picking it up, I learnt it was from Mogadishu and I was instructed to participate in the summit instead of President Mohamed Siad Barre. I immediately went to Airport in order to go to Cairo.

When I came to the foreign ministry in 1982 as vice minister I was unhappy because I preferred to remain in the ministry of Justice. The foreign ministry environment was new to me and I did not know the minister well. Anyway, I accepted the role with the right attitude and soon learnt the foreign services. I found it particularly interesting to learn of the supporting countries and those that did not support Somalia

Also acknowledging, which countries helped us in developing politics, education, health, economy and security. It took me about a year to become familiar with all the countries learning who we had good relations with and those we did not.

Not knowing, that what was in front of me was a Diplomatic Dilemma. I learnt that foreign policy is not dependent only on the people who worked in the foreign ministry but also the president and the cabinet, as it was their role to decide what the foreign policy would be and what direction it would go in. The Somali delegation consisted of myself as Minister of State for Foreign Affairs in Somalia, Ambassador Abdurrahman Farah Ismail, Director General of Arabic Department and Ambassador Abdullah Hassan Mohamud, who was the Somali Ambassador in Cairo.

To make a decision in my position was not easy as I had to make it on behalf of my country. Therefore the responsibility and accountability weighed heavily.

As the head of the delegation, I tried to contact the office of the President, but in vain. Nor could I find the president or other high ranking officials who could share the responsibility. Because of this situation, I did the following; to take balance between the two groups, I needed to ascertain who was the heavy weight? Where was the interest of our country and our people? This interest may be: political, economic, social or security in order to obtain this balance, I brainstormed and decided to do what is right.

I remember that day very well; for Arab League and Arab nations split into two segments. Luckily, I knew which group we were to support. Before this we were one of the opposition groups in the Arab league and so, I had to weigh up the best course of action. I had looked at the two groups and considered the pros and cons. Above all, there is an aggressor and victim. As a lawyer I know of justice and injustices. Therefore, I supported the victim; otherwise the law of jungle would prevail, meaning the big fish will eat the small fish. After, the summit I went to the embassy with Ambassador Abdullah Hassan Mohamud, who was the Somali Ambassador in Cairo. From the Embassy we contacted Mogadishu and fortunately this time we spoke to the President and informed him as to what happened. His answer was explicit and pragmatic (there is no need to narrate is what he stated.). The following day there were protests against the position that we had taken. The reality of the situation was serious. As I heard when I returned to Mogadishu, the cabinet of ministers discussed the matter but the Prime Minister (His Excellency Brigadier General Mohamed Ali Samatar) declined to make a decision. He said: we had sent a delegation, to participate at the summit, let the delegation come back and we would hear their report before that time, it is unlawful to make a decision". I am not stupid; I had done something for my country and my people which satisfied me. Modesty does not allow me to say more than this and the case closed. With that position, I shifted Somalia from left to right. The States which were opposed to supporting Kuwait expelled their citizens from the Gulf countries, while Somali citizens in the Gulf States were welcomed. The Somali passport became the only passport that allowed people to find a job.

President Mubarak wasted no time in dispatching forces to Saudi Arabia. The first of 30, 000 Egyptian troops began arriving on 11 August. Morocco followed shortly afterwards with a symbolic contingent of between 1, 000 and 1, 200 troops (a 5, 000 man unit had been stationed in the UAE since 1986). The arrival of Syrian troops was especially significant in political terms, given Syria's traditional posture as the standard bearer of pan-Arabism and resister to American primacy in the region. Participation made the anti-Saddam coalition more than a club of conservative, pro-Western regimes. By the end of the year, there was a breakdown of Arab armed forces. Deployed in Saudi Arabia under a Saudi-headed unified command was as follows: Egypt 30 000;

Syria 17, 000; Morocco 1, 000 to 1, 200; Kuwait 3, 000 to 5, 000 and approximately 3,100 Egyptian troops. The Moroccan and Syrian contingents were also deployed in the UAE. With Saudi Arabia's 45,000-manned force included, the total number of Arab ground combat troops taking part in the international coalition against Iraq was approximately 100,000. (Dave, 2006)

Chapter eleven

ECONOMIC HISTORY OF SOMALIA

To analysise the Somali economy, we need to talk about five stages; the Colonial era and economic development (1960 to 1969), scientific socialism (1970 to 1975) the socialist revolution post 1975 and the agreement between the Somali government and IMF in 1981 to 1990.

The colonial Era: this period did not offer foreign investment despite the competition of the three major European powers in Somalia—Italy controlled southern Somalia, Britain northern Somalia, and France the area that became Djibouti. Italian parliamentary opposition restricted any government activity in Somalia for four years after European treaties recognized Italian claims in the early twentieth century; projects aimed at using Somalia as a settlement for Italian citizens from the crowded homelands, failed miserably. Although in the early 1930's Benito Mussolini dew up an ambitious plan for economic development the actual investment was modest.

There was still less investment in British Somaliland, which British India administered. During the prime minister ship of William Edward Gladstone in 1880's, it was decided that the British Indian government should be responsible for administering the Somaliland protectorate because the Somali coast's strategy location on the Golf of Aden was important to British India. The biggest investment by the British colonial government, in its three quarter of a century of rule, was in putting down the rebellion of dervishes. In 1947, long after the dervish war of the early 1900's, the entire budget for the administration of the British protectorate was only £213,139. If Italy's rhetoric concerning Somalia outpaced or exceeded performance, Britain had no illusions about its protectorate in Somaliland. At best, the Somali protectorate had some strategic value to Britain's eastern trading empire, to protect the trade route to Aden and British India and assuring a steady supply of food for Aden.

Banana plantations: The two major economic developments of the colonial era were the establishment of plantations, in the Inter Riverine area and the creation of an official salaried class. In the south, the Italians laid the basis for profitable export— oriented agriculture, primarily in bananas and through the creation of plantations and irrigation systems. In both the north and the south, a stable petty bourgeois class emerged. Somalis thus became civil servants, teachers, soldiers, petty traders in coastal cities and small business proprietors.

The plantation system began in 1919 with the arrival in Somalia, of Prince Luigi Amedeo of Savoy, Duke of Abruzziand with the technical support of the fascist administration of Governor Cesare Maria de Vecchi de Val Cismon. Shebelle Valley was chosen as the site of the plantations because for most of the year the Shebelle River had sufficient water for irrigation. The plantations produced cotton (the first Somali export crop) sugar and bananas. Banana exports to Italy began in 1927, and gained primary importance in the colony after 1929, when the world cotton market collapsed. Somalian bananas could not compete in price with those from the Canary Islands but in 1927 to 1930, Italy passed laws imposing tariffs on all non-Somali bananas.

These laws facilitated Somali agricultural development so that between 1929 and 1936 the area under banana cultivation increased seventeen fold to 39.75Km2. By 1935 the Italian government had constituted a Royal Banana Plantation Monopoly (Regia Azienda Monopolio Banana RAMB) to organize banana exports under state authority. Seven Italian ships were put at RAMB's disposal to encourage the Somali banana trade. After World War II, when the United Nations (UN) granted Italy jurisdiction over Somalia as a trustee territory, RAMB was reconstituted as the Banana Plantation Monopoly (Azienda Monopolio Banane - AMB) to encourage the revival of a sector that had been nearly demolished by the War. In 1955 a total of 235 concessions held more than 453KM2 (with only 74Km2 devoted to bananas) and produced 94 000 tons of bananas. Under fixed contracts, the three banana trade associations sold their output to the AMB which exacted an indirect tax on the Italian consumer by keeping out cheaper bananas from other sources. The protected Italian market was a mixed blessing for the Somali banana sector. Somali bananas made possible the initial penetration to the international marketplace beyond Italy.

Cotton: The investment in cotton showed fewer long term results than the investment in bananas. Cotton showed some promise in 1929 but its price fell following the collapse in the world market. Nearly 1, 400 tons in 1929 exports, shrank to about 400 tons by 1937 and during the trustee period, there were years of modest success. In 1952 for example, about 1, 000 tons of cotton was exported however there was no consistent growth. In 1953 exports dropped by two-thirds and two reasons are given for cotton's failure as an export crop; an unstable world market and the lack of Somali labour for cotton harvesting.

Co-participation contracts with Somali farmers; the Italians received sole purchasing rights to the crop, in return for providing seed, cash advances and technical support.

Sugarcane: sugarcane was more successful. The sugar market differed from the banana and cotton in two respects: sugar was raised for domestic consumption and a single firm, the Italo – Somali agricultural Society (Societa Agricola Italo- Somalia SAIS) with its headquarters in Genova, controlled the sector. Organized in 1920, the SAIS estate near Giohar had by the time of the trustee period, a little less than 20KM2 under cultivation. In 1950 the sugar factory's output reached 4,000 tons enough to meet about 80 % of domestic demand. By 1957 production had reached 11,000 tons and Italian Somaliland no longer imported sugar.

Labour shortages beset Italian concessionaries and administrators in all plantation industries. Most Somalis refused to work on farms for wage labour. The Italians at first began compulsory enlistment of people who lived in the agricultural region. Later, Italian companies paid wages to agricultural families to plant and harvest export crop and permitted them to keep private gardens on some of the irrigated land. This strategy met with some success and a relatively permanent work force developed.

Somali plantation agriculture was of only marginal significance to the world economy. However banana exports reached US $6.4 million in 1957; cotton US$ 200, 000. and in 1957 plantation export constituted 59 % of total exports, representing a major contribution to the Somali economy.

The colonial period also involved government employment of salaried officials and the simultaneous growth of a small urban bourgeoisie. In the north, the British administration originally had concentrated on the coastal area for trading purposes but soon discovered that livestock to be traded came from the interior.

Therefore, it was necessary to safeguard caravan routes and keep peace in port areas, requiring the development of a police force and other civil services. In British Somaliland many of the nomads scorned the work so consequently only a small pool, of literate Somalis were available to work for the British administration in the south. Somalis sent children to colonial and mission schools and the graduates found civil service positions in the police force as customs agents, bookkeepers, medical personnel and teachers. These civil servants became a natural market for new retail business, restaurants and coffee shops. Baidoa in the pre-colonial period had almost no permanent commercial sector. By 1945, nearly 500 businesses were registered in the district of Baidoa alone and these urban Somalis challenged colonial rule.

Economic development 1960 to 1969: with independence, the Somali economy was at a near survival level, with the new state lacking the administrative capacity to collect taxes from subsistence herders and famers. The state could rely on the customs taxes from international trade as they were easier to collect. However, tariffs failed to meet the needs of the government with their ambitious development goals. Therefore Somalis relied on Italian and British subsidies which funded about 31% of the new nation's current budget in the first three years of independence. Somalia also received grants and loans from countries in the East and the west. This made possible the articulation of an ambitious development plan by 1963. A five year plan with a budget of more than US $100 million in grants and loans focusing on investment in infrastructure. The plan's proposal was that plantation crops and livestock export would increase if there were better roads, transportation facilities, ports and irrigation works. Another large investment was made in the creation of model farms to attract farmers from around the country, who would learn improved techniques to apply on their own farms. Model farms in Baidoa Region, Afgooye near Mogadishu and Tog Wajaale, west of Hargeysa were established during this period.

Livestock: In the pastoral sector, the Livestock Development Agency, formed in 1965—1966, emphasized veterinary service, the provision of water and of holding grounds for cattle while they were undergoing vaccination and transportation. Somali pastoralists responded with enthusiasm to the prospects of wealth by entering the international market for livestock. In the early 1960's, the value and number of exported livestock approximately doubled and livestock soon surpassed bananas as Somalia's leading export.

There were some notable successes among Somalia's early development projects with the nation becoming nearly self-sufficient in sugar and banana as exports grew although haltingly. Livestock exports increased and investments in roads and irrigation facilities resulted in some genuine improvements.

But the country could not overcome its dependence on foreign assistance even to meet its current budget. Moreover, imports of foreign gains increased rapidly, indicating that the agricultural sector was not meeting the needs of the growing urban population. The modern agricultural techniques of state farms had little influence on traditional farming practices. Because of a boom in livestock export from Hargeysa, cows, goats and camels were becoming more concentrated in northern Somalia, much to the detriment of rangelands. Finally and perhaps most importantly, many Somalis lacked interest because of the belief that the political incumbent through electoral manipulations, were wasteful of the nation's economic resources for their private benefit.

Scientific Socialism 1970 to 1975

Siad Barre legitimated his 1969 coup d'état in terms of the national economic optimism. On October 20 1970, on the first anniversary of the coup, he announced.

"In our Revolution we believe that we have broken the chain of a consumer economy based on imports and we are free to decide our destiny. And in order to realize the interests of the Somali people, their achievement of a better life, the full development of their potentialities and the fulfillment of their aspirations, we solemnly declare Somalia to be a Socialist State."

The revolution announced the 1971—73 Three Year Plan. The plan emphasized a higher standard of living for every Somali, jobs for all who sought work and the eradication of capitalist exploitation. Agriculture 'crash programs' and creation of new manufacturing plants were the immediate result.

The revolution quickly brought a substantial proportion of the modern economy under state control. The government nationalized banks, insurance companies, petroleum distribution firms and the sugar refining plant and created national agencies for construction materials and foodstuffs. Although the Somali neologism for socialism, hantiwadaag could be translated as the sharing of livestock - camel herds were not nationalized and Siad Barre reassured pastoralists that hantiwadaag would not affect their animals. To mollify international business, in 1972 Siad Barre announced a liberal investment code and because the modern economy was so small, nationalization was more showmanship, than a radical change in the economy.

Creation of cooperatives

The creation of cooperatives soon became a cornerstone in building a socialist economy. In 1973 the government decreed the Law of Cooperative Development with most funds going into the agricultural sector. In the pre coupe years, agricultural programs had received less than 10% of total spending. By 1974, the figure was 29.1% however the investment in cooperatives had limited long-term results. In

Galole near Hargeysa for example, a government team established a cooperative in 1973 and government funds helped purchase a tractor, a cooperative centre and a grain storage tank and members received token salaries as well. But in July 1977 with the beginning of the Ogaden war, state involvement in Galole ended; by 1991 the cooperative was no longer in operation.

Cooperatives also aimed at the nomad although on a smaller scale. The 1974—78 Development Plan allocated only 4.2% of the budgeted funds to livestock. Government officials argued the scientific management of rangelands—the regeneration of grazing lands and the drilling of new water holes—would be possible only under socialist cooperation. In the fourteen government-established cooperatives each family received an exclusive area of two to three kilometres of grazing land and in times of drought common land under reserve could become available. The government committed itself to providing educational and health services as well as serving as a marketing outlet for excess stock and neither agricultural nor fishing cooperatives proved economically profitable.

Integrated agricultural development projects were somewhat more successful than the cooperatives. For example, the Northwest Region Agricultural Development Project survived the 1980's. Building upon the bunding (creation of embankment to control the flow of water) constructed by the British in the 1950's and also by the United States Agency for International Development (USAID) in the 1960's. The World Bank picked up the program in the 1970's and 1980's. Yields from bunded farms increased between 24 and 137.4 t/km over the yields from unbunded farm showed overall improvement in agricultural production was hardly noticeable at a macrocosmic level.

Somalia's rural-based socialist programs attracted international development agencies. The Kuwait Fund for Arab Economic Development (KFAED) USAID and the FAO participated first in the Northern Rangelands Development Project in 1977 and in the Central Rangelands Project in 1979. These projects called for the rotating of grazing areas using reserves and creating new boreholes but the drought of 1974 and political events undid most efforts.

During 1974-75 a drought devastated the pastoral economy. Major General Husseen Kulmiye headed the National Drought Relief Committee, which sought relief aid from abroad among other programs. By January 1975 China, the United States, the European Economic Community, the Soviet Union, Italy, Sweden, Switzerland, Sudan, Algeria, Yugoslavia, Yemen and others had pledged 66, 229 tons of grain, 115 tons of milk powder and tons of other food products. Later that year with aid from the Soviet Union, the government transported about 90, 000 nomads from their hamlets to agricultural cooperatives at Duujuma on the Jubba River (about 180 km), Kurtun Waareyc near the Shebelle River (about 60 km) and Sablaale northwest of Chisimaio (about 60 km). The KFAED and the World Bank supported irrigation projects in these cooperatives, in which corn, beans, peanuts and rice were planted. Because the government provided seeds, water, management, health facilities, schools, as well as workers' salaries, the farms were really state-owned farms rather than cooperatives. Essentially, they became havens for women and children because after the drought, the men went inland with whatever money they had accumulated to buy livestock to replenish their stock of animals.

The government also established fishing cooperatives. Despite a long coastline (3, 025 kilometres) and an estimated potential yield of 150, 000 tons per year of all species of fish, in the early 1970s fishing accounted for less than 1% of Somalia's gross domestic product. In 1975 cooperatives were established at Eyl, a post in the Nugaal region; Cadale, a port 1,200 kilometres north east of Mogadishu; and Baraawe. The Soviet Union supplied modern trawlers; when Soviet personnel left Somalia in 1978 and Australia and Italy supported these fishing projects. Despite their potential and broad-based international support, these cooperatives failed to become profitable. The revolution emphasized the great economic successes of the socialist experiment, a claim that had some truth in the first five years of the revolution. In this period, the government reorganized the sole milk-processing plant to make it more productive. They also established tomato-canning, wheat flour, pasta, cigarette and match factories and a plant that manufactured cardboard boxes and polyethylene bags and established several grain mills and petroleum refineries. In addition, the state put into operation a meat-processing plant in Chisimayu as well as a fish-processing factory in Laas Qoray, northeast of Erigavo. The state worked to expand sugar operations in Giohar and to build a new sugar-processing facility in MARARAY so progress in the early socialist period was not uniform. The government heralded various programs in the transport, packaging, irrigation, drainage, fertilization and the spaying? of the bananas and despite the boom year in 1972, banana exports declined.

The socialist revolution after 1975

Popular enthusiasm for the revolution began to dissipate by the mid-1970s. Many officials had become corrupt and used their positions for personal gain. In addition, a number of ideologues had been purged from the administration as potential threats to their military superiors. Perhaps most important, Siad Barre's regime was focusing its attention on the political goal of liberating the Ogaden (Ogaadeen) rather than on the economic goal of socialist transformation. The Somali economy was hurt as much by these factors and by the economic cost of creating a large modern army as it was by the concurrent drought. Two economic trends from this period were noteworthy: increasing debt and the collapse of the small industrial sector.

During the 1970's, foreign debt increased faster than export earnings and by the end of the decade, Somalia's debt of 4 billion shillings equaled the earnings of seventy-five years of banana exports (based on 1978 data). About one third was owed to centrally planned economies (mainly the Soviet Union, US $110 million; China, US$87.2 million; with small sums to Bulgaria and the German Democratic Republic (East Germany). Another one third of the debt was owed to countries in the Organization for Economic Cooperative and Development (OECD). Finally, one-third was owed to members of the Organization of the Petroleum Exporting Countries (OPEC) (principally Saudi Arabic, US$81.9 million; Abu Dhabi, US$67.0 million; The Arab Fund for Economic and Social Development, US $34.7 million; Kuwait, US $27.1 million; and similar amounts to Iraq, Qatar and the OPEC special account, Libya and Algeria, in that order. Many loans, especially from the Soviet Union, were in effect, written off and later, many loan repayments to OECD states were rescheduled. But thanks to the accumulated debt burden by the 1980's the economy could not attract foreign capital and virtually all international funds made available to Somalia in rescheduling agreements came with the provision that international civil servants would monitor all expenditures. As a result of this international debt, Somalia lost control over its macroeconomic structure.

A second ominous trend in the 1975-81 periods was the decline of the manufacturing sector. Exports of manufactured goods were negligible when the 1969 coup occurred; by the mid 1970's, manufactured goods constituted 20% of total exports. In 1978, as a consequence of the Ogaden War, exports were almost non-existent and production likewise suffered. In 1969 Somalia refined 47,000 tons of sugar; by 1980 the figure was 29 100 tons (all figures are for the fiscal year). In 1975 the country produced 14.4 million cans of meat and 2 220 tons of canned fish. In 1979 it produced 1.5 million cans of meat and a negligible amount of canned fish. Textile output rose over the period but the only material produced, was a coarse fabric sold to rural people (and worn by the president) at less than cost. In milk, pasta, packaging, materials, cigarettes and matches, the trends were downward in the second half the 1970s.

The agreement between the Somali government and IMF 1981 to 1990

With its socialist program in disarray and the alliance with the Soviet Union lost in the wake of the 1977-78 Ogaden War, Somalia once again turned to the West and like most countries devastated by the debt in the late 1970s, Somalia could rely only on the nostrums of the IMF and its program of structural adjustment.

In February 1980, a standby macroeconomic policy agreement with the IMF was signed but not implemented and the standby agreements of July 1981 and July 1982 were completed in July 1982 and January 1984 respectively. To meet IMF standards, the government terminated its policy of acting as the last-resort employer of all secondary school graduates and abolished its monopoly on grain marketing. The government then prepared a medium-term recovery program consisting of a public investment program for 1984-86 and a phased program of policy reforms. Because the International Development Association (IDA) considered this program too ambitious, the government scaled down its projects most notably the construction of the Baardheere Dam which AID had advised against. The government abandoned its first reform program in 1984 and in March 1984, the government signed a letter of intent accepting the terms of a new US$183 million IMF extended credit facility to run for three years. However in a Somali Council of Ministers meeting in April, this agreement was cancelled by one vote as the soldier—ministers chafed at the proposed 60% cut in the military budget. The agreement also called for a further devaluation of the shilling and reductions in government personnel.

A new crisis hit Somalia in June 1983 when the Saudi Arabian government decided to stop importing Somalia cattle and this ban soon expanded to include sheep and goats. Saudi officials claimed that rinderpest had been detected in Somali livestock making them unsafe. Cynics pointed out that those Saudi businessmen recently had invested in Australian ranches and were seeking to carve out an export market for their product. In any event the ban created a large budget deficit and arrears on debt started to accumulate. A major obstacle to expanding livestock and other exports was Somalia's lack of communications infrastructure: good roads and shipping facilities as well as effective telecommunications and postal services. Lack of banking facilities also posed a problem Somalia could not easily avoid the medicine of structural adjustment.

In March 1985, in negotiations with the Paris Club (the informal name for a consortium of eighteen Western Creditor countries) Somalia's debt service schedule was restructured and the government adopted a reform program that included devaluation and the establishment of a free market for foreign exchange for most private transactions. In November 1985 in conjunction with the Consultative Group of Aid Donors (a technical body of the Paris Club) the government presented its National Development Strategy and Programme with a revised three year investment program. Western aid officials criticized this program as too ambitious. In June 1986 the government negotiated an agricultural sector adjustment program with IDA and in September 1986, foreign exchange rates applicable to different types of transactions consequently came into existence. AID prepared a second-stage project report in 1986 that renewed the call for privatization and it praised the government for permitting the free importation of petroleum products but chided the Somalis for not yet allowing the free marketing of hides and skins. AID put great pressure on the government especially by means of lobbyists, to take action on legislation to permit banking. To encourage the private sector further AID was prepared to fund the Somali Chamber of Commerce if the Somali government would allow it to become an independent body. The 1986 report went beyond privatization by calling for means of improving the government's revenue collection and budgetary control system. Building a government capable of collecting taxes, making policy reforms and addressing fiscal problems became the new focus. Along these lines AID encouraged the elimination of civil service jobs and as in 1985 5,000 civil servants had been dismissed and AID felt that 80% of the civil service was still redundant however AID officials urged pay raises for those in useful jobs.

Somalia's Five-Year-Plan for 1987—91 largely reflected the international pressures and incentives of the IMF and AID and privatisation was written into the plan as were development projects that were smaller in scale and most easily implemented. By 1988 the government had announced implementation of the IMF and AID-encouraged structural adjustment policies. In regard to foreign exchange, the government had taken many intermediate steps that would lead to the merger of the pegged and market rates. As for banking, legislation had been enacted allowing private banks to operate in public finance and the government had reduced its deficit from 10 to 7% of GDP, as they had been advised but acknowledged that the increased taxes on fuel, rent and sales had been only partially implemented. A value-added tax on fuel imports remained under consideration but the tax on rental income has been increased and the sales tax raised from 5 to 10%. The government continued to procrastinate, concerning public enterprises holding only informal discussion of plans to liquidate unprofitable enterprises. With the devaluation of the shilling, the real cost of foreign grain became apparent to consumers and the relative price of domestic grain rose rectifying prices induced a 13.5% increase in agricultural output between 1983 and 1985. Inflation was tamed as well, falling from an annual rate of 59% in 1980 to 36% in 1986 and World Bank officials used the data to publicize the Somali success in structural adjustment.

The overall picture was not that encouraging as manufacturing output declined, registering a drop of 0.5% per annum from 1980 to 1987. Exports decreased by 16.3% per annum from 1979 to 1986 and the 0.8% rise in GDP per annum from 1979 to 1986, did not keep up with the population growth. Work Bank estimates put Somalia's 1989 GNP at US$1,035 million or US$170 per person and further estimated that between 1980 and 1989 real GNP per person declined at 107% per year.

In the period from 1987 to 1989, the economic results of agricultural production were mixed. Although corn, sorghum and sugarcane were principal crops, livestock and bananas remained major exports. The value of livestock and banana exports in 1989 (the latest year for which data were available in May 1992) was US$26 million and US$25 million respectively. Livestock, consisting primarily of camels, cattle, goats and sheep, served several purposes. The animals provided milk and meat for domestic consumption livestock, hides and skins for export. As a result of the civil war in many areas the economy deteriorated rapidly in 1989 and 1990. Previously livestock exports from northern Somalia represented nearly 80% of foreign currency earned until these exports came to a virtual halt in 1989.Shortages of most vital commodities including food, fuel, medicines and water occurred virtually countrywide. Following the fall of the Siad Barre regime in late January 1991, the situation failed to improve because clan warfare intensified.

Mineral sector: Surveys were done by the Department of Geology of the Somali National University or the Russians (previously the Soviet

Union) identified some valuable deposits of minerals though the minerals were not developed for production and export. By 1988, the mineral sector constituted only a tiny percentage of the GDP, equal to 0.3% despite the potential that minerals could have helped Somalia to generate hard currency needed for meeting the demands of its public. The mining sector of Somalia is virginal and over the years it was neglected and ignored. With immense potential there are countless options and opportunities to those who intend to invest in Somalia in the future. The geological evolution of Somalia together with abundance of mineral deposits and its diversity are pointers towards rich and massive potential destined for discoveries. Unexploited deposits include: Gold, anhydrite, bauxite, columbines, copper, feldspar, iron ore, silica and, tantalum and uranium.

Conclusion

Somalia gained independence in 1960. Before that time, it was colonized by three major Europeans powers: British, France and Italy. During this period there was no meaningful economic development. The two major economic developments of colonial era were:

- The establishment of plantation of bananas in the Inter- River area.
- The creation of a salaried official class.

The Italians paved the way through the creation of plantation and irrigation systems in 1919 so when Prince Luigi Amedeo arrived and selected the site of this plantation on Shebelle Valley, for the most of the year there was sufficient water for irrigation. The first plantation produced was cotton, therefor cotton was the first Somali export crop, then sugar and bananas followed by ample livestock knowing that there is adequate demand for meat internationally and fisheries; Somalia has the longest coast in Africa, there were numerous varieties of fish. There is sufficient land to be cultivated for different varieties of crops that could be exported to international markets. Therefore, Somalia is not a poor country, but it required foreign investment. (Metz, 1993)

Author's Biography

MOHAMED ALI HAMUD

Childhood

I was born in the district of Tieglow, Bokool 13 April 1940, into a family of half nomads and half farmers. My father was a soldier in the Italian colony, his name was Ali Hamud Abdi and my mother was Hawa Ma'alin Ali, she died when I was five years old so was raised by my father and my elder sister Hawa Ali Hamud. I finished my education at the Qur'an school in Tieglow.

I felt the absence of my mother and remember how I suffered by not having her present as other children had although my elder sister tried to be a good substitute, she could not replace my Mother.

What could I do we all walk with destiny. Psychologists define the mother as the person in whom, life receives a form suitable for living in the world. What does it mean living in this world, it means that a person is alive and functioning physically and spiritually. It means that a person hungers for physical as well as spiritual nourishment and loving others and being loved by them, establishing intimate, committed and growing relationships, appreciating culture and nature and most of all loving and worshipping the Creator. All these begin to take shape and grow in the person as they grow inside their mother. Therefore they say there is mother earth and the earth plants grow and give physical nourishment to the rest of God's creatures and in mother places of worship, such as a Mosque or a Church, a person is born again by the Holy Spirit so as a result when I lost my mother, I suffered.

When I turned six years old, my father took me to Qur'an school in Tieglow. The teacher of the Qur'an school was my uncle from my mother's side. Apparently, I was a smart student and one evening the teacher's mother saw that the teacher was beating me. I was being punished because I helped another student, who had made mistakes in memorizing the Qur'an. When the teacher went home, she scolded him and said, "How dare you beat your sister's son, knowing that his mother died and he is an orphan". Later on my uncle, Sheikh Hassan Hamud, who was a Judge in Luuq Ganane, asked his brothers (Ali Hamud my father and Ibrahim Hamud my uncle) to send to him any smart young children. They had decided to send me to him, along with my uncle's son Mohamed Ibrahim Hamud. Therefore, my uncle Ibrahim Hamud took us to our uncle Sheikh Hassan Hamud when I was fourteen in 1953. This was the first time that we went to an actual school! We were in Luuq for months, until my uncle was transferred to Lower Juba (Chismaio). My uncle Sheikh Hassan was a democratic man and he never imposed his ideas on anybody and always gave each a chance to give his/her opinion. He was conservative and well educated in Islamic Juridical therefore, he called us; Mohamed Ibrahim Hamud and myself and asked if we would be willing to go with him to Chismaio or we could choose to return to Tieglow. I decided to go with him to Chismaio, Mohamed Ibrahim chose to return back home to his parents. For me, a poor boy, it was best to go with my uncle, which was excellent; our God guided me and mentored me in the right way and we went to Lower Juba (Chismaio). I did not know anything about the Somali people, how divided they or where they settled. During the trip to Chismaio, when we were passing at Shallanbout near Merca, it was the time to pray so we stopped. On the side of the road there were many ladies who intended to go to Brava, Gilip Gemama, and Chismaio. They spoke the language of Brava and Bajuni, I had not heard this language and wondered about it! Then I asked my uncle, 'Uncle where we were going?" my uncle laughed and said we are in Somalia, these languages you hear are Brava and Bajuni, from now on you will hear these languages and when we reached Chismaio we tried to find a house to rent and got one in the centre of city.

It was in 1954, during this time I was studying the Italian language at primary school and was fifteen years old and enthusiastic to learn, so I attended the morning and afternoon classes. I could understand

Italian but could not speak it and I was very good at mathematics. My teacher in the afternoon, a young Italian lady, noticed that I needed to improve the language, so she proposed to my uncle to give me to her, in order to teach me more. My uncle rejected the proposal, saying that this boy is my trustee, I cannot give him to you as he is my brother's son and my uncle remained in Chismaio for two years.

One day while we were in the afternoon class, the teacher asked me to explain something from the Arabic language and I did not know the language and told the teacher, the children in the class laughed at me however they did not know my dialect. The teacher became angry and scolded them and asked, "Why are you laughing? this dialect is spoken in the next district, to Chismaio". I became very angry. In 1956, my uncle was transferred to higher Juba (Baidoa) and as a man of eighteen years, I could read and write both the Italian and Arabic languages so my uncle wanted to make me his clerk in the court. I was keen so he suggested to me that I select a girl in Baidoa to marry and I thanked my uncle for his proposal but at that time, I didn't have any intention of marriage so I told him, that if you are to pay me money to get married, I would prefer that money for my education, as I need to learn. I had thought a lot about my future and I was independent and determined by nature. My relationship with my father was a distant one; I had no knowledge of him and did not know if he was alive or dead. I decided to run away to Mogadishu in order to try and get a chance at self-education. When we were going to Chismaio and passed Mogadishu I had seen some students wearing a uniform and was bright and clean thus I was eager to wear one like that, one day. I dreamt of that day and I wanted to realize it.

Adolescent

Mogadishu was the Capital from 1957 until 1965 while living there, I was in my Uncle's home. Living there as well were two other relatives both were unemployed and other people residing, who rented rooms from my uncle. My life was at stake - where was I to get food? I was forced to find a job and worked by washing clothes earning sh. 5 a day and it was enough to survive on and later on I found a better job, this time I worked as a waiter in an Italian house and I was earning sh 150 a month.

This interfered with my desire to study and unfortunately there was nobody to guide me, accept my God and what is better than God's guidance? I trusted my capacity; I knew that if I had an opportunity I could achieve good results. So, I joined a school in Ma'alin Jamac's primary school, this is now women's House in front of National theatre.

One day at school, we were outside and there was a loud noise followed by confusion. We didn't know what happened and I was put in charge of the class, as the teacher told me to look after it while he went to find out what happened and upon returning the teacher told us "That one Egyptian dog had been killed "

For the rest of the day, I asked myself what did that mean? I did not know what Egyptian was so when school finished I went to the home of one of my relatives who explained it to me.

I used to see the Egyptian man who was killed, making speeches at the Somalia party meetings as he was one of the representatives of UN who was controlling and supervising the Italian Trusteeship in Somalia. He was active in that role and attended all parties meetings and his name was Mohamed Kamal-Aladdin.

On this day I changed my mind about that school because of the disrespect for the poor man who was killed.

One day, while I was working I saw some young people gathering in front of a building and asked them what they were waiting for? and they told me it was for an admission examination to the school so I asked if I could also do the exam and they said, yes I could, as there no pre-conditions.

I completed the exam and passed but later a problem arose because these young people were part of a specific political party. Placed on the notice board was a list containing the names for attendance at the school and my name was not included so was rejected and could not join the school. I was angry again, all those students, wearing the uniform that I admired so much, whom may I go, in order to solve this problem I wondered? I asked one of my relative's and he suggested that this evening we should go to a man who he thought could help as this man worked for my relative so we went and were received. When we explained the situation, he said to me, "Tomorrow morning at 8am be at the front of the school and we will do what we can". The next day went together into the office of the Director, that man who was well known at the school and a member of the school committee.

The Director said that the committee did not allow for the inclusion of people not from the political party so my friend said, "Did you open this school for the political party members or for the young people of Somalia?"

The response was "yes, we opened it for all, young Somalis".

"Therefore, this young boy will come tomorrow to attend this school".

From that day forward I found what I was looking for in education. This school was my primary school for four years then I continued to high school and finished in 1965. I then secured a scholarship to study in Egypt with fifteen other students from my school. Before we went to Egypt, they told me that I was to go to the faculty of English literature however I only wanted to study law. I asked my favourite English teacher (Ibrahim Al Makripi and he said, "Mohamed if you want to know of justice, you must go to the faculty of law". I applied to join the faculty of law and luckily when we arrived in Cairo, they told me that I was registered in law at Alessandria University. Our fifteen students were scattered to different faculties, one other boy joined me and we remained there for two years.

When the war broke out between Egypt, Syria and Jordan against Israel, in June (5th to 10th), in 1967 (the Six-day war) this was a big setback for all three countries. We sat for examinations in those confusing times and most of the students failed, due to the effect of the defeat. In 1968 I shifted from Alessandria to Cairo, to continue my studies at the Cairo University faculty of law. I remained in the faculty for three years and completed my degree in 1970. During my study I thought a lot about my future and worried because of what was going on in my country. There was much nepotism, corruption and mal administration. I knew when I went back it would not be easy to find a Job. Therefore, I considered going to foreign countries to seek a Job.

Luckily, the Somalia coup d'état occurred on 21/10/1969. We heard from our country national songs that said "The problem now in Somalia is not whom you know, it is what you Know", meaning it is not who you know that will get you somewhere in life but what you have learnt, a graduation could make your dreams come true. As soon as I had my degree I returned home and I remembered the day I arrived in Mogadishu, it was 28/7/1971. Conscription had become law as set up by the Supreme Revolution Council (SRC). Therefore, every student who returned from abroad was obliged do military training at the Halane camp. So, for three months we went to the Police school.

The happiest years of my life

This period from 1971 to 1976 were amongst the happiest years for my life and passed the entrance examination held by Ministry of Justice. This was while I was at the military training camp of Halane. Can you guess my salary - it was Sh.1500! This was more than enough for a big family. After I ended the military training, I went to the ministry of Justice and began work at the District Court of Mogadishu as a Judge. This was until 1973, from where I was nominated as President of the Court of Appeal in Mogadishu. I remained there until 1976.

The experience I gained from the justice system

During the time I worked in the ministry of justice (from 1972 to 1980) are two relevant cases that I judged.

Case One
Court of District: Haig Ali Self- represented vs The Queen, The Judge and Mohamed Ali Hamud

The incident for this case happened in Mogadishu in 1964, when I was in high school. It remained in the District court system without being trialed for eight years. When I joined the ministry in 1972 they allocated me to the district court of Mogadishu as a judge. When I arrived at the court, I met the president of court, Sheikh Hussen. After two weeks the president assigned me the case. When I studied it, I found the case consisted of dozens of papers. I was astonished as the case was about a conflict between a Sufis and a fanatical group. One member of the fanatical group, Hagi Ali, insulted a well-respected man who passed away. They called him Manaqib, which is a Sufi name.

This case I soon learnt was a critical one and one previous judges were afraid to touch it so it remained on the shelve of the district court for eight years. As you may know, most Somali people believe in the Sufism creed (Dariqa). I hesitated but thought, if I do not judge it, who will? I had graduated from the faculty of law and the other Judges were not as well qualified as I was. After careful consideration, I decided to judge the case irrespective of the result. The first session of the court started at 9.30am and the people of Mogadishu came early to the court so when I arrived I could not enter, it was so full and I was afraid. I had to instruct the police to remove the crowd who had gathered in front of the court and the hall of the court was jammed-packed.

The testimony began and it was very complicated. I recognized that the case was dangerously explosive so I bought in two experts in Islamic religion. These two experts I knew very well, they had both graduated from Al-Azhar University and they accepted the nomination.

They were; Sharif Abdinur and Sheikh Mohamed Nu Abdurrahman.

After a week they submitted their findings to the court and these were excellent; they concluded that "The outstanding traits (manaqib) are not part of Qur'an, but the author of outstanding traits is one of the famous Sharif, who died a long time ago"

There was a clause in the Somali penal code that stated if someone offended dead people they would be penalized for six months or fined Sh.600.

In making the decision, the court took the following into consideration:
- the sensitivity of the case because of the Sufism creed
- to minimize the sensitivities and feelings.

The verdict

To fine Hagi Ali, the offender Sh. 600. His sentence satisfied both sides and for these reasons:
- the Sufism; because the offender received a penalty
- the fanatics; because the Sufism had been told that the outstanding traits were not a part of the Qur'an.

I Thanked God for his guidance because the case ended in peaceful way.

Case Two

Court of Appeal: The appellant the buyer Self- represented vs the respondent the camel herder Self- represented

This case took place in the BARCO Region and I will never forget this case because it showed the greed of human beings which I will summarize it the following pages.

This case happened near the district of Odwayne, in the BARCO Region. There was a man who was a herder who raised camels and one night whilst he was travelling a young camel could not stand up as it had an Achilles heel problem; this was because the season was in famine. As he knew a well to do man who lived close by, he went to see him and told him the story. This man was very kind and he proposed that he would buy the ailing camel so he herder accepted the generous offer of sh. 150. And the herder took the money and continued on his way. The Buyer raised the animal, it was female who produced five calves. When the herder learnt of this, he returned to the buyer and asked him for more money. The buyer gave him another Sh.500 and he asked him to pray to God to bless his animal. Two more calves were born, increasing the total to seven calves. When the herder learnt of this, he decided to sue the buyer.

The herder went to the regional court, saying that the camel had disappeared from his pack a long time ago, and then found it among in this man's herd. Therefore, he wanted to claim back his camel and the court judged in favour of the herder.

The buyer took the plea to the court of Appeal of BARCO. At the time I was the president of the Court of Appeal in BARCO so I looked into the case and called the parties to session. I heard from the herder that he had lost the animal and found it amongst the animals of the buyer. The litigant (the buyer) then narrated the history as it was and at that point I asked the herder if he had witnesses, to prove his claim he said he did. I gave him thirty days to produce these witnesses and after thirty days, he came to court without a witness saying in front of the court, that the witness had travelled beyond the Somali border and he couldn't find him. I gave him thirty days again, in order to bring the witness in. I told him, do not worry about the expenses the court will cover these. After thirty days, again he returned to the court without his witnesses Knowing that the buyer brought the camels to the court each time it was in session, at great expense, I at this point told the parties that the court would decide the case. After one week, I gave judgment in favour of the buyer. The reason was the herder deviated from justice, and did some double-dealing with the law and I told the herder, that he has the right to appeal to the high court in Mogadishu after thirty days. When the thirty days were up he returned to court ready to appeal in Mogadishu. He told the clerk that he wanted to see the judge and I was suspicious about his intentions so I called the police and the clerk to come with him, into my office. When they came the herder said, "Your honour you had delivered justice therefore I am not going to appeal but I do ask for your kindness, to cancel the expenses". I told him "That it is not my right to cancel the expense as this is the responsibility of the appellate, let me ask the appellate for a decision". We called the appellant, who was worried the case would be taken to the high court, we explained to him the respondent's offer which and after explaining this to him, he accepted in a good manner. Therefore I was able to cancel the expenses.

Later, I wondered why did this man commit all these claims and cause the other people to suffer? Is this the nature of human beings? No doubt he was greedy and ruthless. The buyer was generous and did a good deed for him, by buying the weak camel and gave him a generous 150 Sh. later, he gave him another 500 Sh.. Yet his reward was to be sued..

Curriculum Vitae

MOHAMED ALI HAMUD

Address: 34/5 Pearcedale Pde, Broadmeadows VIC 3047, Australia
Email: mohamedhamud35@hotmail.com
Nationality: Somali and Australian
Contact number: +61434266097

Education background

2004 –2005 : Master of Public Management Griffith University Australia

1966 – 1970: Bachelor of Law from Cairo University Egypt

1960 –1965: High school from Gamal Abdi El-Nassir Somalia

Employment history

1991 – 1993: Minister of Foreign Affairs —Interim government

1980 – 1990: Member of Parliament

1982 – 1990: Minster of State for Foreign Affairs

1982 – 1983: Vice Minister of Foreign Affairs

1980 – 1982: Vice Minister of Justice and Religion affairs

1972 - 1973: A Judge at the District court in Mogadishu

1973 – 1976: President of the Court of Appeal Mogadishu

1976 – 1977: President of the Court of Appeal Burco and Sanag regions

1978 – 1980: President of court of appeal of Jowhar Middle Shebelle

Books written by the author during the period of the civil war are the following:

1. The civil war in Somalia, its causes and effects (1992) written in Arabic.
2. The Golden years of Somalia, written (2013).

Languages: Somali, Arabic, English and spoken Italian.

Reference

Dr. Andre Le Sage (2005), Stateless Justice in Somalia centres for Humanitarian Dialogue R. 2009-06-26.

Helen Chapin Metz, Somalia: a country study, (The Division: 1993), p.10

Horn of Africa Journal, 1997, vol. 15, Issues 1-4, p.130, Horn of Africa.

I.M. Lewis (1988) A modern History of Somalia nation and The State in the Horn of Africa, West View Press.

ISS, 2005, Political History, Retrieved From http://www.iss.co.za/AF/profiles/Somalia/Politics.html

Johns, Dave, 2006, "1990 the Invasion of Kuwait". Frontline/World. PBS. Retrieved on March 2012 From http://www.pbs.org/frontlineworld/stories/iraq501/events_kuwait.html

Luling, Virginia (2002). Somali Sultanate: the Geledi city-state over 150 years Retrieved From http://en.wikipedia.org/wiki/Geledi_sultanate

Naval History and Heritage Command, 'The Potsdam Conference, July - August 1945', Retrieved From http://www.history.navy.mil/photos/events/wwii-dpl/hd-state/potsdam.htm

Tripodi, Paolo, 1999 The Colonial Legacy in Somalia. p. 66

Wikipedia, 2013, Ajuuraan state, Retrieved From http://en.wikipedia.org/wiki/Ajuuraan_state

Wikipedia, 2013, British Somaliland Retrieved From http://en.wikipedia.org/wiki/British_Somaliland

www.ingramcontent.com/pod-product-compliance
Lightning Source LLC
Chambersburg PA
CBHW032042290426
44110CB00012B/923